Arado Ar 232 A-0 V1 (Werk-Nr. 232 0001, GH+GN) with retracted caterpillar undercarriage during testing. The aircraft, with fairings for the main undercarriage, was photographed in June 1942 still without camouflage, markings and armament.

Arado Ar 232 "Tatzelwurm"

Dr. Jörg Armin Kranzhoff

Reconnaissance aircraft of the Royal Air Force began monitoring activities at the Rechlin Proving Station in 1942. On 28 April 1943, specialists assessing aerial photographs of the station obtained using a new reconnaissance method came upon two unusual and previously unknown German aircraft. What they were looking at was a type of transport aircraft that had never existed before. They were Ar 232 A-0 pre-production aircraft, early examples of a rough field transport aircraft whose design set standards that remained trend-setting even after the end of the war.

Arado broke new technical ground with the Ar 232. The company's first large aircraft had been the Arado VI, developed at the end of the 1920s. It delivered record performances as an express mail plane with the airline Luft Hansa, but because of the company's tight financial situation development was not pursued. After that Arado's largest aircraft was the Ar 77 twin-engined trainer, which was built around 1935.

The Ar 232 design sprang from the pen of Wilhelm van Nes, who became head of the Arado design bureau (TEW) during a restructuring of the company in 1935 and steadily gained influence compared to the previous head of development Franz Meyer, who had come from Albatros in 1932. In 1938 the firm's original technical director, Walther Rethel, also left Arado to become head of the Messerschmitt design bureau. Following this, van Nes and the young aerodynamicist Rüdiger Kosin were largely responsible for the company's new designs.

Van Nes was born in Freiburg, Breisgau on 26 September 1900. After serving in the First World War, from 1919 to 1924 he studied mechanical engineering and natural science at the Stuttgart Technical School and the University of Freiburg. After

Ar 232 A-0 V1 seen from above, June 1942.

earning his degree he became a team leader in the structural office of the Heinkel-Werke in Warnemünde. From 1926 to 1927 he was part of the Guritzer - van Nes Aircraft Company in Salzburg. He subsequently worked as a scientist and from 1929 to 1931 was a design engineer at Albatros. There he worked with Walter Blume, who joined Arado in 1932 and assumed control of the company after it was nationalized in 1936. In 1942 van Nes was named a corresponding member of the German Academy of Aviation Research in recognition of his accomplishments.

In autumn 1939 Arado, Fieseler and Henschel were issued a development contract for a medium transport to replace the obsolescent Ju 52. During the occupation of the Netherlands it was seen how easily the enemy had rendered landing surfaces unusable with simple means, resulting in heavy losses among the transport units, and in late 1940 the RLM modified the development contract, specifying a "rough field transport for use near the front".

Arado subsequently designed the Ar 232 transport under the project number E 440. The aircraft was to be capable of rough field operations, with the lowest possible takeoff and landing speeds and short field capability. Designed for a crew of four, the transport was supposed to be able to transport bulky, heavy loads over a distance of about 1500 km to the immediate vicinity of the front, be loaded and unloaded quickly, and be capable of disassembly for transport by rail.

A design description dated 24 January 1941 envisaged a cantilever high-wing monoplane of stressed skin, monocoque construction with a low-slung fuselage and a spacious cargo hold behind the cockpit with a length of 6.6 meters, a clear width of 2.3 meters and a height of 2 meters. An internal overhead crane was envisaged for loading. The aircraft's estimated gross weight was 15000 kg with a normal payload of 2300 kg. It was to be capable of hauling 4800 kg in overloaded condition, equivalent to 48 fully equipped troops or an equivalent weight in heavy equipment. The rear part of the fuselage floor could be lowered hydraulically to serve as a loading ramp or be opened in flight to drop cargo or parachute troops. In contrast to the Henschel design, which had twin tail booms and was eliminated from the competition in the project phase, the aft fuselage of the Arado transport consisted of a slender tail boom comprised of two half shells. It was attached to a frame in the aft fuselage and the rear spar and was positioned high so as not to interfere with loading. The tail section was divided, with twin fins and rudders. The cantilever tailplane was set on the tail section bearer, which was designed to accommodate a towing plate for gliders.

Power was to be provided by two BMW 801 A air-cooled, 14-cylinder, two-row radial engines each producing 1,560 hp (1150 kW). They operated on the four-stroke principle with fuel injection and had a two-stage supercharger. The engines had reduction gearing for VDM three-blade propellers with automatic pitch control and a diameter of 4.2 meters.

The three-piece, twin-spar wing consisted of a one-piece rectangular center section which housed the leak-proof fuel tanks and the undercarriage. Attached to this were the two trapezoid-shaped outer wings. The use of a high-lift wing previously tested on the Ar 80 with extendable hinged flaps significantly reduced takeoff and landing distances.

The Ar 232 A-0 handbook described the arrangement of the flaps, or "landing wings", as follows:

> "Located on the wing center section on either side of the fuselage there is a landing flap consisting of a light metal framework and a torsionally-stiff sheet metal leading edge. It has metal skin on top and fabric skin on the bottom and is hinged on two rails. The outer wings are fitted with flaps tapering toward the tip. The individual flaps consist of a single-spar light metal frame with torsionally-stiff leading edge, with metal skinning top and bottom. They are the length of the aileron, have a closed nozzle box behind the spar and are hinged on two booms."

The flaps were extended and retracted hydraulically and could be lowered by hand crank in the event of a loss of electric power. There was also an emergency lowering system for the tricycle undercarriage, which was normally operated electro-hydraulically. It was one of the first of its type to be used on a German aircraft and was designed for prepared airfields.

The aircraft earned the nicknames "Tatzelwurm" or "Tausendfüssler" (millipe-

de) on account of its second undercarriage, with which it could take off and land on uneven ground with a reduced payload. Thought was originally given to a version with a rubber crawler belt, however a so-called "multi-wheel undercarriage" subsequently proved the better solution. The landing impact was absorbed by the oil-damped kneeling tricycle undercarriage. Because of its size it was capable of considerable shock absorption and caused a certain compression of the ground. By retracting the nosewheel and shortening the oleos of the main undercarriage, the aircraft could be lowered to the level of the roller undercarriage situated 60 cm higher. This consisted of a double row of low-pressure balloon tires mounted on swing arms with shock absorbers. After lowering, the transport could be loaded easily.

Ar 232 A-0 with extended landing flaps on 10 June 1944, with members of the Arado Flugzeugwerke design team, which had been relocated to Landeshut, Silesia. Wearing the pale flight suit in the bottom row is company pilot Jakob Kunz, next to him on the left head of Design Bureau I Hans Rebeski and on the right the head of Design Bureau II Walter Föhring. Photo: Hans Rebeski

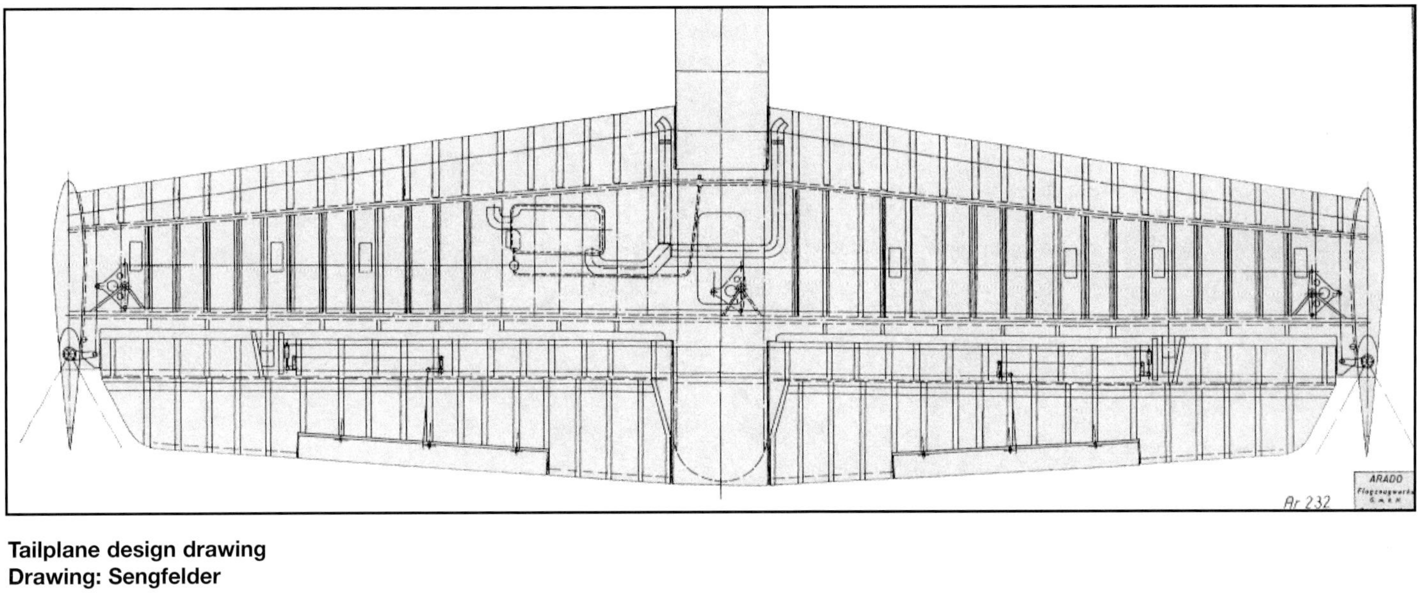

Tailplane design drawing
Drawing: Sengfelder

Ar 232 A-0 photographed in Orel, Russia during the winter of 1943-44. As an operational aircraft, it was equipped with a machine-gun turret above the cockpit.

In initial trials, which were conducted in a hangar, lowering of the fuselage from a crane hook worked flawlessly. During flight trials, lowering tests were conducted on a specially-built obstacle field. It was found that the fuselage could only be lowered after the aircraft began to move, as additional forces affected the aircraft from the front during engine run-up. It was found that the lower shock strut of the system developed by Kronprinz tended to jam because the guide length was insufficient. In order to address this shortcoming as quickly as possible, modifications were made based on verbal directions from the design department. These involved increasing the insertion depth of the lower shock strut.

Arado documents reveal that the Ar 232 was considered especially for special missions in North Africa and the Arctic. The envisaged equipment sets included winter and tropical equipment, a radio system, an inflatable dinghy, oil-fired heating, an emergency electrical power generator and snow skis on shock absorbers for weather reconnaissance in the Arctic. Experiments by the Office Group LC 2/FP on 26 September 1941 revealed that snow skis with wooden bottoms were stronger than metal skis. Whether these skis were actually built and put to use is not known. Other equipment included gun positions with MG 81Z machine-guns in the nose, atop the fuselage and in the tail. Window mounts could also be installed in the cargo hold for lateral defense. In October 1943 towing trials were also conducted with DFS 230 and Gotha Go 242 gliders. The trials were successful, however the gain in payload was marginal and the idea was abandoned.

A memorandum dated 14 February 1941 reveals that two prototypes of the twin-engined A-0 pre-production series and a structural airframe for ground testing were supposed to be built. Priority was given to completing the required drawings, which were supposed to be delivered by April. The target date for completion was October-December 1941. Parts design began on 30 March 1941 and the first mockup inspection took place on 26 May. Calculations for mass distribution and center of gravity position were carried out in June 1941.

The aircraft's complicated technology led to an extended testing period. An RLM message dated 10 October 1941 reveals that strength testing of the main undercarriage had not yet been completed. On 7 May 1942 the company held discussions concerning modifications related to the blowing systems for the wing and flaps. The Ar 232 V1 (Werk-Nr. 232 0001, GH+GN) flew for the first time in Brandenburg on 28 June 1942. According to Delivery Plan No. 21 of 1 February 1942, its purpose was engine testing and general trials. Normal flight testing lasted until 25 September 1942. On 28 August the V1 was demonstrated to representatives of the RLM in Brandenburg. The V1 was first test-flown in Rechlin on 3 September 1942. The aircraft returned to the factory in January 1943, mainly for undercarriage testing. On 29 October 1943 a pilot from Rechlin flew the V1 back to the proving center, where for the next three months it underwent a thorough program to test the undercarriage. The final entry is dated 12 January 1944. There is no mention of the Ar 232 V1 in Delivery Plan No. 225 of 24 April 1944.

According to Delivery Plan No. 21, the Ar 232 V2 (Werk-Nr. 232 0002) was supposed to initially take part in general trials. Although doubts were expressed that it was in fact the V2, this prototype was probably also used in trials of the boundary layer control procedure. It was originally planned that takeoff-assist rockets should be used to shorten the Ar 232's takeoff distance. It was envisaged that a braking parachute or braking rockets would be used to shorten the rollout after landing. The demand for an increase in payload and the associated increase in takeoff distances led to the search for new lift-increasing technologies. For this reason the Ar 232 V2 was supposed to be fitted with a boundary layer extraction and blowing system, with which it was hoped a maximum lift coefficient of 4.0 could be achieved.

Starting point was the question whether the level of the max-lift point in the area of the wing profile's leading edge radius could be maintained farther back on the airfoil through appropriate measures. Investigations in the wind tunnel in the AVA Göttingen revealed that an energy supply over a slot along the leading edge of the aileron or flap pivot area in a spanwise direction represented a solution. A Walter motor in each wing was supposed to bleed the boundary layer from the landing flap area and blow it out again over the aileron area. Aerodynamicist Friedrich Wagner was placed in charge of the experiments.

In July 1941 Arado was already awaiting delivery of a test system from the aerodynamic research institute in Göttingen. It was considered tested and ready for use. A design description titled "Ar 232 with suction wing" dated 20 February 1942 confirms the planned "installation of bleed and blow system with elimination of the Fowler flaps" in a wing mockup. There was a reference to such tests in Delivery Program No. 222 of 1 November 1942. Dated May 1943, correspondence with Hirth in Zuffenhausen for the delivery of a small gas turbine reveals that the bleed system was not yet operational. According to Delivery Plan No. 225 dated 24 April 1944, the Ar 232 V2 was then in the company's hands and was again to be employed in testing the boundary layer control system until the end of April.

Rolf Renatus, then a member of the team working on the bleed procedure, described how it went about putting the Göttingen results to work:

> "The power units used were one gas turbine per wing. To produce thrust they used Walter fuel, which was also used for rocket engines. The bleed air was subsequently blown out again. The gas jet pump had a central nozzle plus a "wreath" of eight more nozzles. All of the nozzles in this pump were designed as supersonic nozzles (Laval nozzles). The gas jet pumps demonstrated their effectiveness on the test bench. As a result, it was possible to confirm the outputs of the propulsion jet produced by the nine Laval nozzles derived from the Göttingen results.

For the carry-over to the Ar 232 the next step was to fix the ratio between the wing areas affected by bleed and blowing on both sides of the wing. In each case the bleed area began near the fuselage, as the most favorable bleed design possibilities were present there.

The gas jet pump was located in the boundary area between the bleed and blow surfaces. All of this first took place in an original wing torso with the space between the rear spar and the profile end and the wing root to the spanwise end. The required mass distribution in a spanwise direction was achieved using known, suitable means and via flexible, cross-section-controlling elements. In this respect the craftsmanship of the "Arado sheet metal artists" is deserving of belated re-

Technical drawing of the elevator.

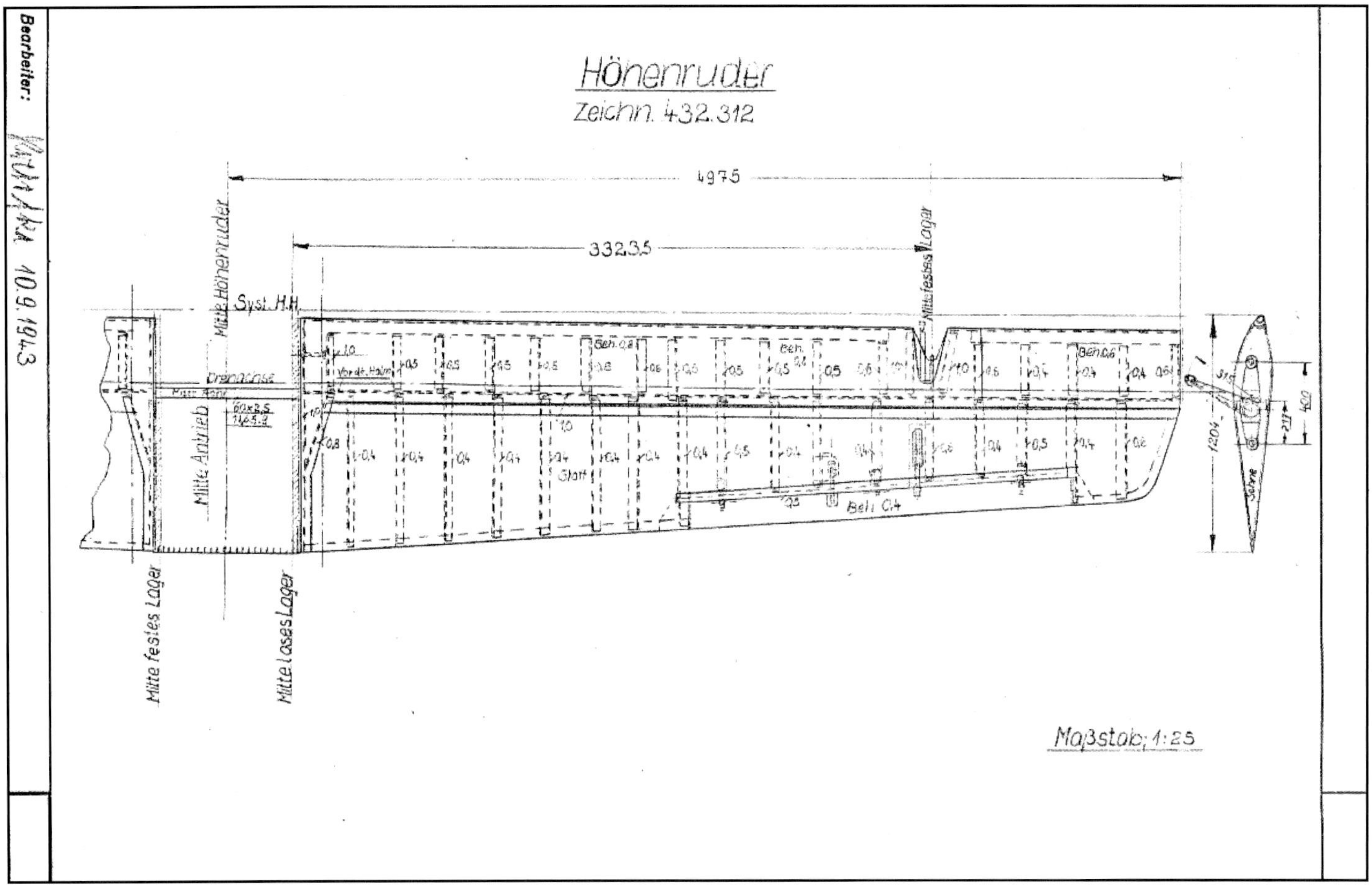

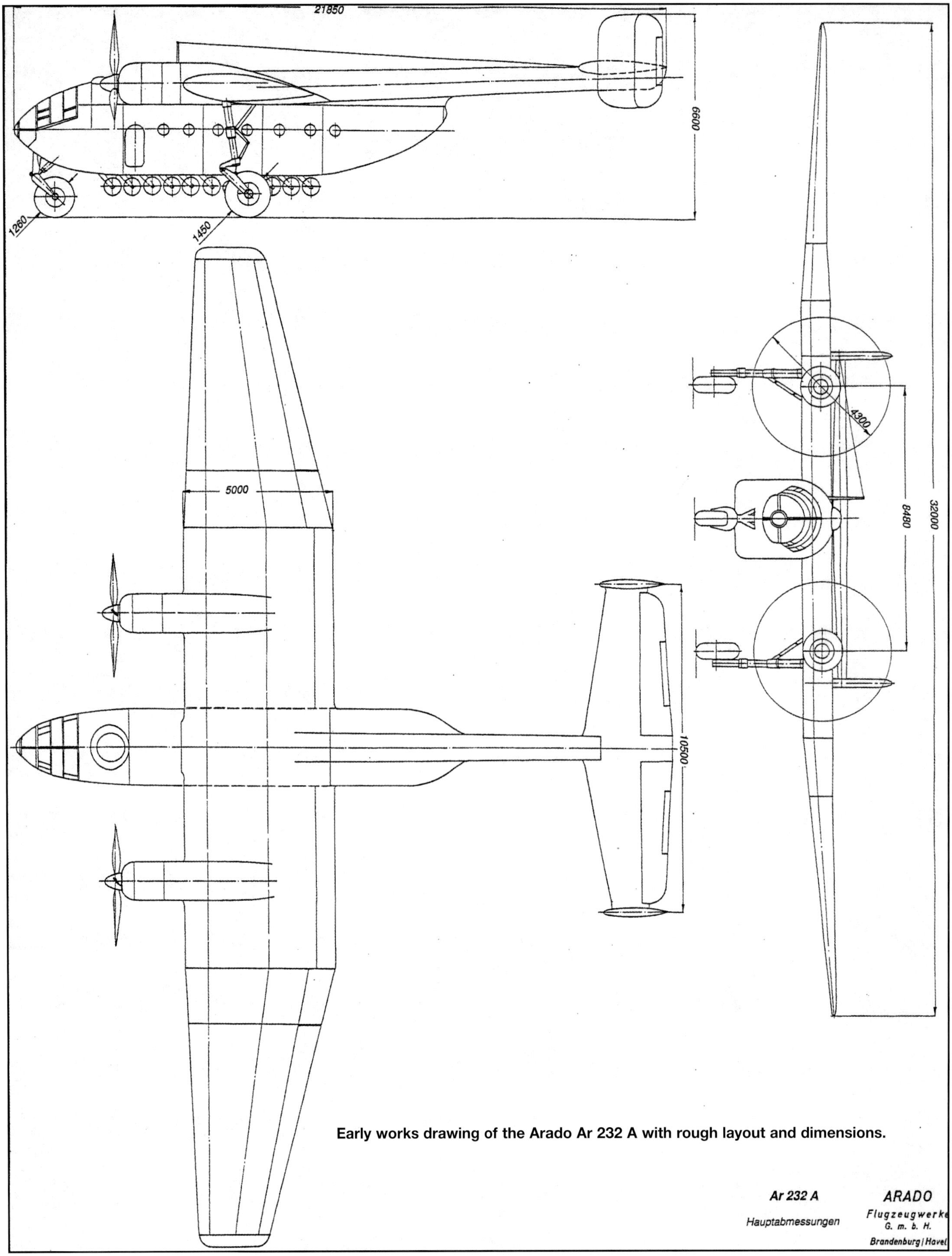

Early works drawing of the Arado Ar 232 A with rough layout and dimensions.

A-0 Series Technical Specification

Wingspan	32,00 m
Length	23,50 m
Height	5,90 m (lowered) 6,60 m
Gross weight	18.500 kg (overload)
Load capacity	7.265 kg (overload)
Payload	4.800 kg (overload)
Gross weight	16.000 kg (normal load)
Load capacity	4.265 kg (normal load)
Payload	2.300 kg (normal load)
Max. speed	305 km/h
Cruise speed	252 km/h
Landing speed	98 km/h
Takeoff distance	445 m (over 20 m high obstacle)
Landing distance	200 m
Service ceiling	7600 m
Range	1500 km
Power plants	2x BMW 801 A with 2x 1560 hp 2x 1300 hp combat power
Armament	1x MG 81 Z (A-Stand) 1x MG 81 Z (B-Stand) 1x MG 81 Z (C-Stand)

cognition with respect to speed and quality. The cylindrical fuel tank with a diameter of about 1.2 meters was sufficient for a takeoff and landing with adequate safety. These experiments took place on the Brandenburg grounds in the summer of 1942."

Rüdiger Kosin recalled that the turbine-powered system powered by Walter T-Stoff originally considered ran into procurement difficulties, as the Walter factory in Kiel was stretched to capacity by navy contracts. As all of the systems described in the technical literature and by the manufacturers appeared totally inadequate, an extensive experimental program was set in motion in cooperation with the high-speed wind tunnel in Göttingen and the Walter factory in Kiel, with the goal of developing a suitable pump. According to Kosin, by 1943 the work had reached the point where a full-size bleed and blow system for the Ar 232 could be tested in Brandenburg, and in the winter of 1943-44 the system was installed in the test-bed. Because of the priority assigned to the flight testing of jet

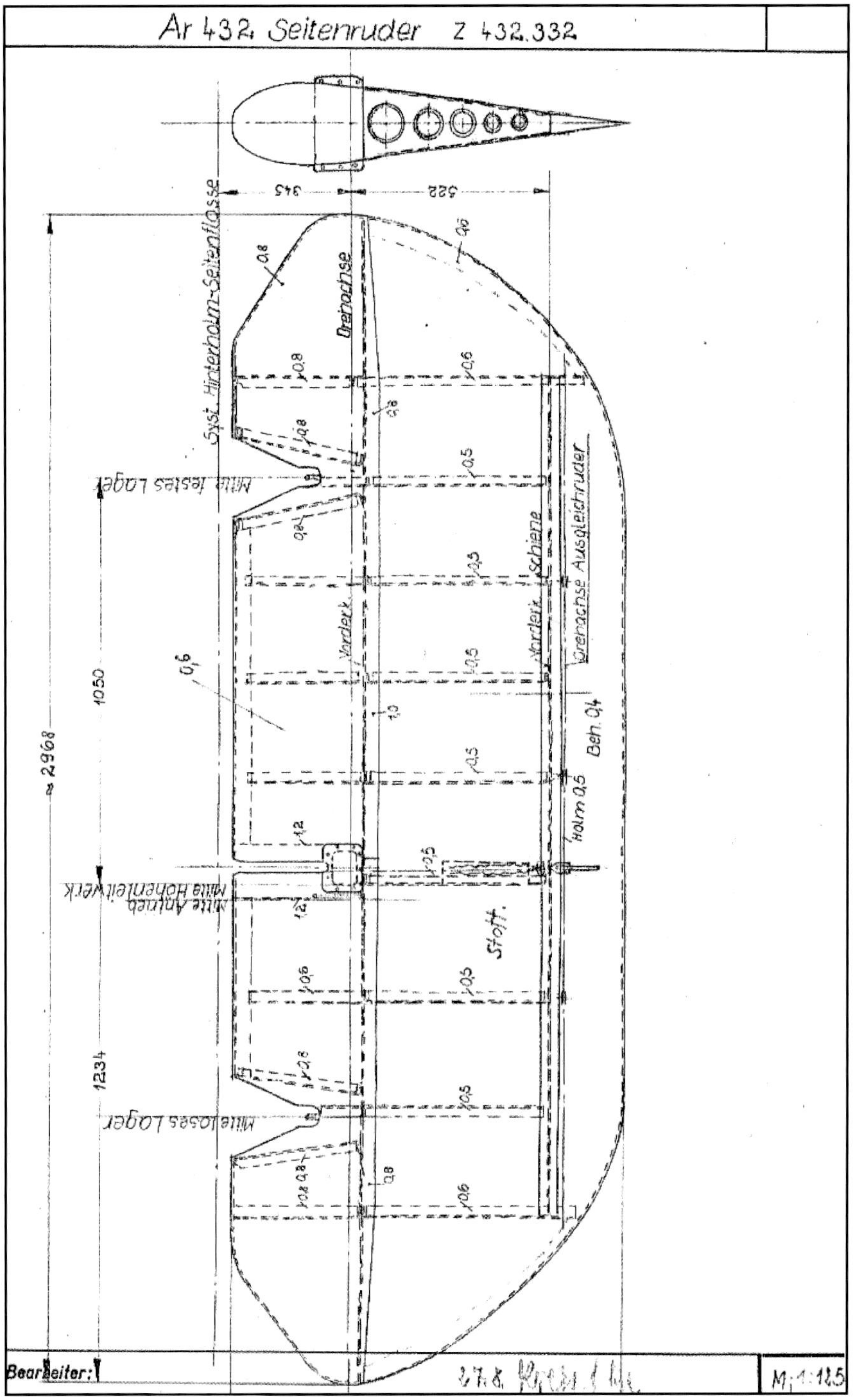

Technical drawing of the rudder.

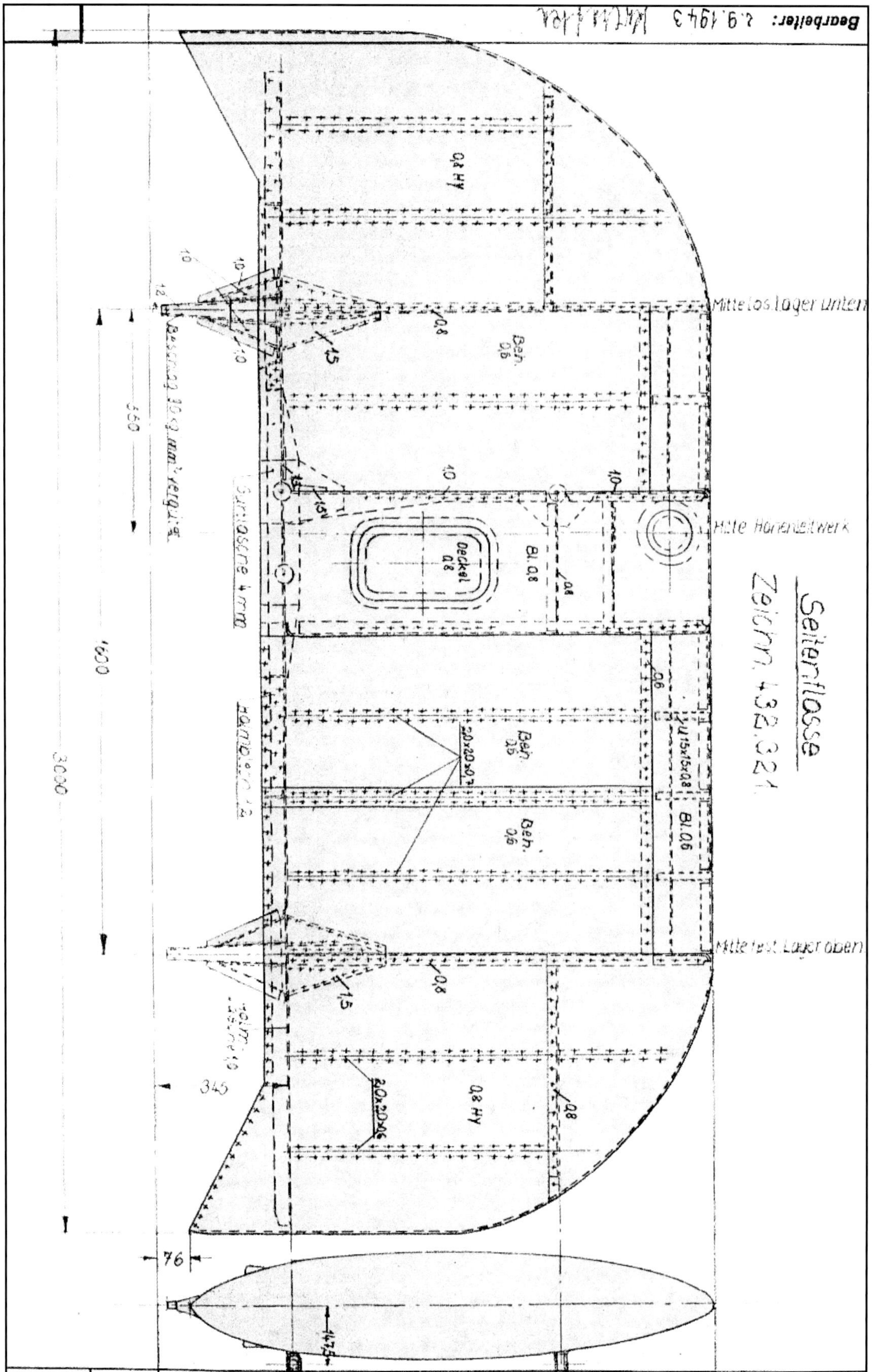

Factory drawing of the rudder.

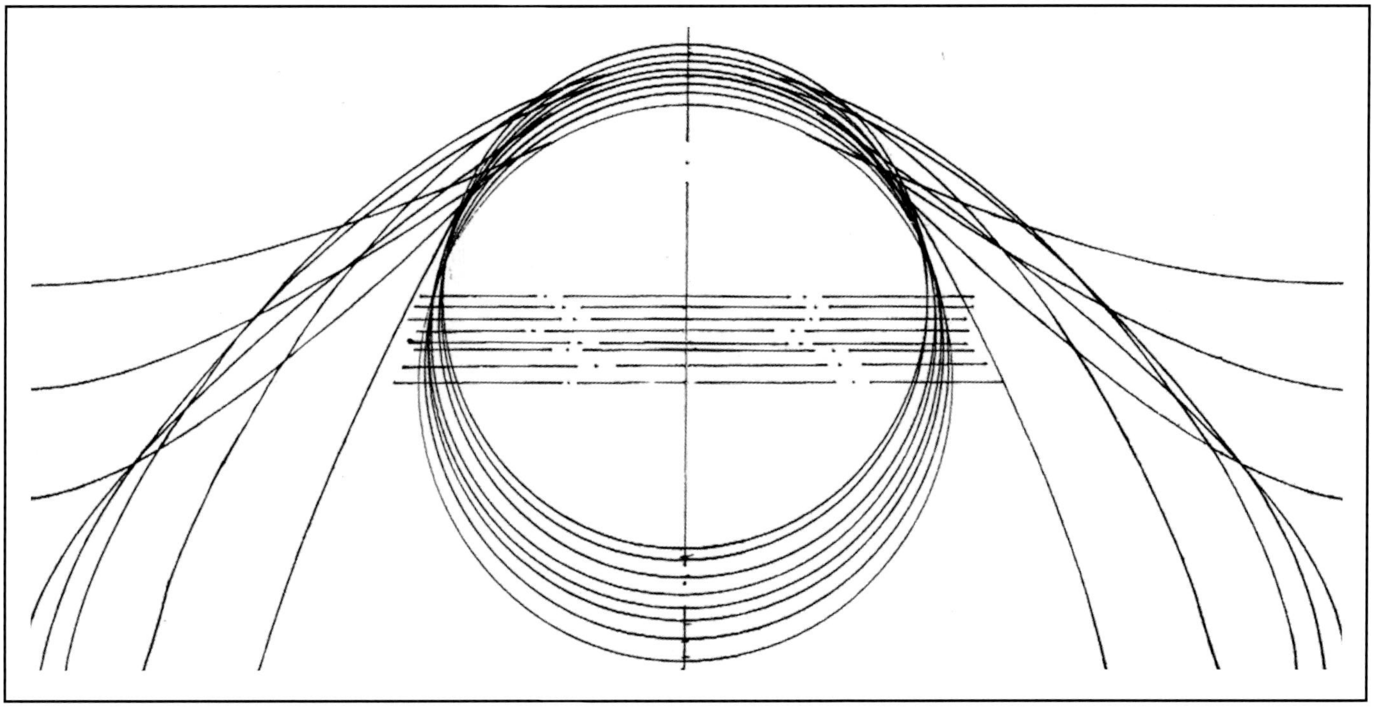

Upper fuselage frame plan.

aircraft, however, testing of the system in flight had to be postponed, and the aircraft was instead used for other, company-related purposes.

The dimensions and weights of the pre-production series Ar 232 A-0 built by Arado were somewhat greater than those of the preliminary design draft. At 32 meters the wingspan was 4 meters greater, and wing area was 135 m² compared to 120 m². With a normal load, gross weight rose from 15 000 kg to 16 900 kg. Because of the open question as to whether the Luftwaffe could afford the highly-advanced transport, there were constantly changing delivery requirements. In February 1941 the company initially assumed that completion of the prototypes would be followed by the construction of 35 A-0 pre-production aircraft at the company's branch plant in Eger. During a meeting on 3 June 1941 it was announced that RLM representative Gottfried Reidenbach would be visiting and that it was expected that he would agree to "the construction of ten examples of the twin-engined Ar 232 A-0 production aircraft". While Delivery Plan No. 19/2 of 1 June 1942 authorized the procurement of materials for 75 examples of the A-1 series, it listed just six zero-series aircraft, to be delivered by December 1942. According to company minutes dated 5 June 1941, ten pre-production aircraft were still planned. After development of the transport was temporarily halted—according to Delivery Plan No. 20 of 15 October 1941—the follow-up program of 15 March 1942 again requested ten examples of the A-0 series. On 15 April 1942, in a meeting with Blume, Generalfeldmarschall Erhard Milch surprisingly declared that the Ar 232 was "of relatively minor importance", and spoke of a "tactical transport" for which only a modest production run was to be expected. In fact, ten examples of the A-0 pre-production series were completed by mid-1943 (Werk-Nr. 010 0003 to 010 0012).

On 6 November 1942 there were clues to suggest that the RLM "had strong interest" in the Ar 232 and that "support" was therefore also to be expected. Walter Blume wanted to "assign the highest priority to testing" and to initiate a "transfer of experience" for the B series.

An Ar 232 A-0 taking off from an unpaved runway.a

Fuselage details
Drawing: Sengfelder

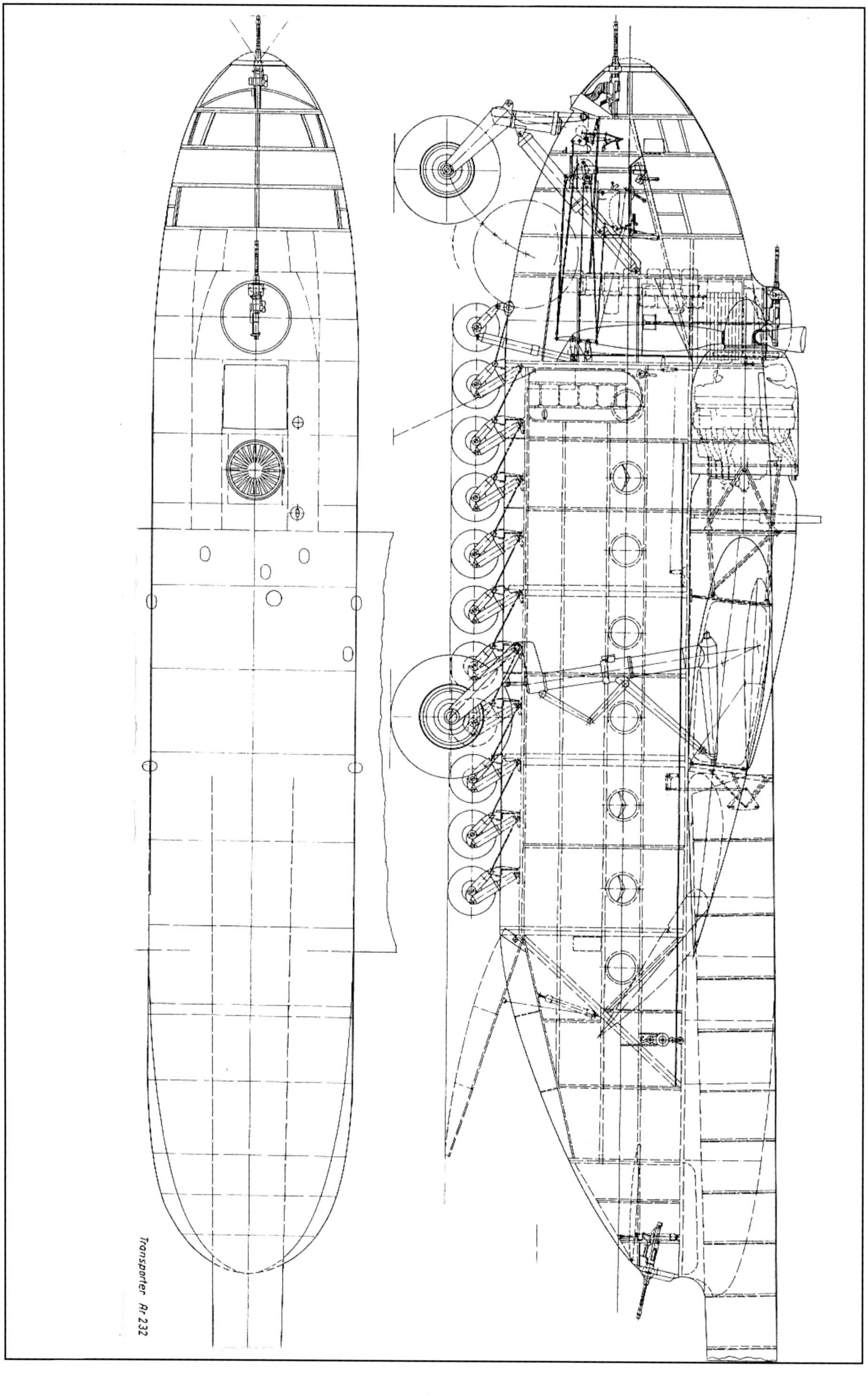

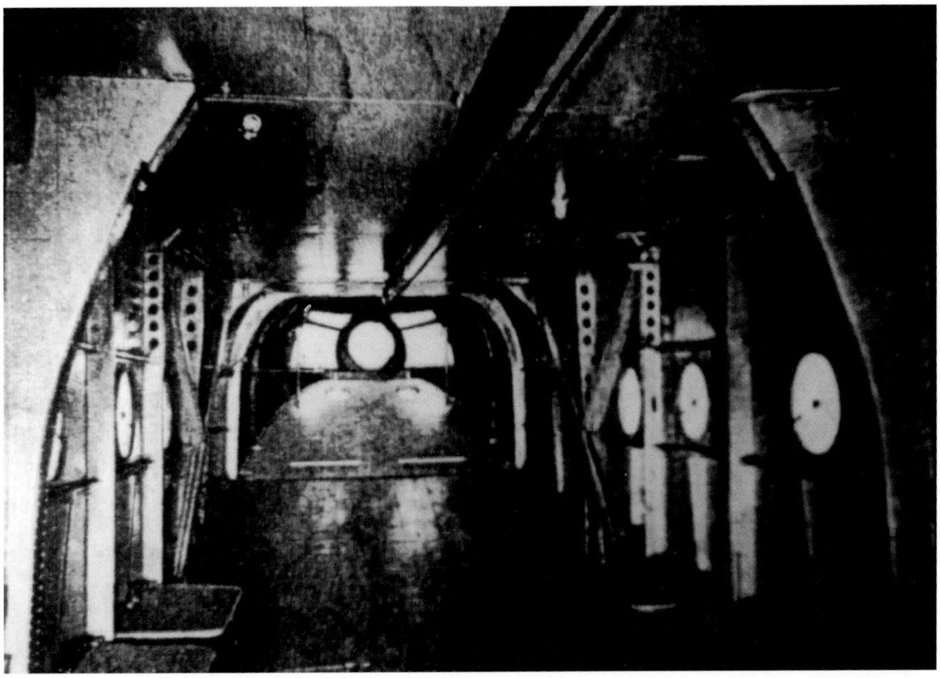

Cargo hold of the Ar 232 V1
Source: Ar 232 A-0 Handbook

In 1943 the production plans for the Ar 232 again proved unrealistic. During a development conference on 7 August 1942, Generalmajor Carl August von Gablenz, head of the planning office, rejected further production of the aircraft. He was of the opinion that the proven Ju 52 could handle most of the tasks envisaged for the Ar 232 and characterized the type as "an aluminum consumer of the worst sort". Fbm. Walter Friedel, head of aircraft development, replied that the special aircraft had been developed at the suggestion of the Technische Amt (RLM Technical Office), that it had met the requirements for rough field capability and a takeoff distance of 100 meters, and that it was ideally suited, especially for winter operations. After Generalstabsingenieur Roluf Lucht concluded the criticism by stating that they "could not afford the machine because of [production] capacity ratios and therefore had to put it on ice", Milch also declared that he would "cancel the aircraft if he could". Ten days later at a meeting of department heads it was decided that a decision would be made within the next three months as to whether the Ar 232 would continue to remain part of the construction program. The minutes noted:

The Technische Amt ordered development of the B-0 with the objective of achieving improved performance. This series was to include development of a float version under the project designation E 401. As the power plants used by the twin-engined Ar 232 A-0 were urgently needed for fighter production, it was decided that the four-engined version would be powered by BMW/Bramo 323 R2 radial engines each producing 1,000 hp (735 kW). The additional engines also improved safety in the event of the loss of an engine. Doubling the number of engines also resulted in a slight lowering of the power loading, from 5.13 kg/hp to 4.38 kg/hp. Payload, on the other hand, dropped slightly, for the increased gross weight of 17 500 kg was the result of the additional engines and the longer 33-5-meter wing, 2.5 meters longer than that of the A-0.

The first two examples of the four-engined version were the Ar 232 B-01 (Werk-Nr. 011 0013, KI+ZT) and B-02 (Werk-Nr. 011 0014), which were built after the last of the ten A-0 pre-production aircraft (Werk-Nr. 010 0012). After a two-month delay, the B-01 took off on its maiden flight on 30 July 1943. In March 1942 an order was placed for 20 Ar 232 B-0 pre-production aircraft. In July of that year the requested quantity was increased to 127 examples of the B-1 series, production of which was to begin in November 1942.

> "As the Ar 232 requires a great deal of development capacity and comes with a heavy use of light

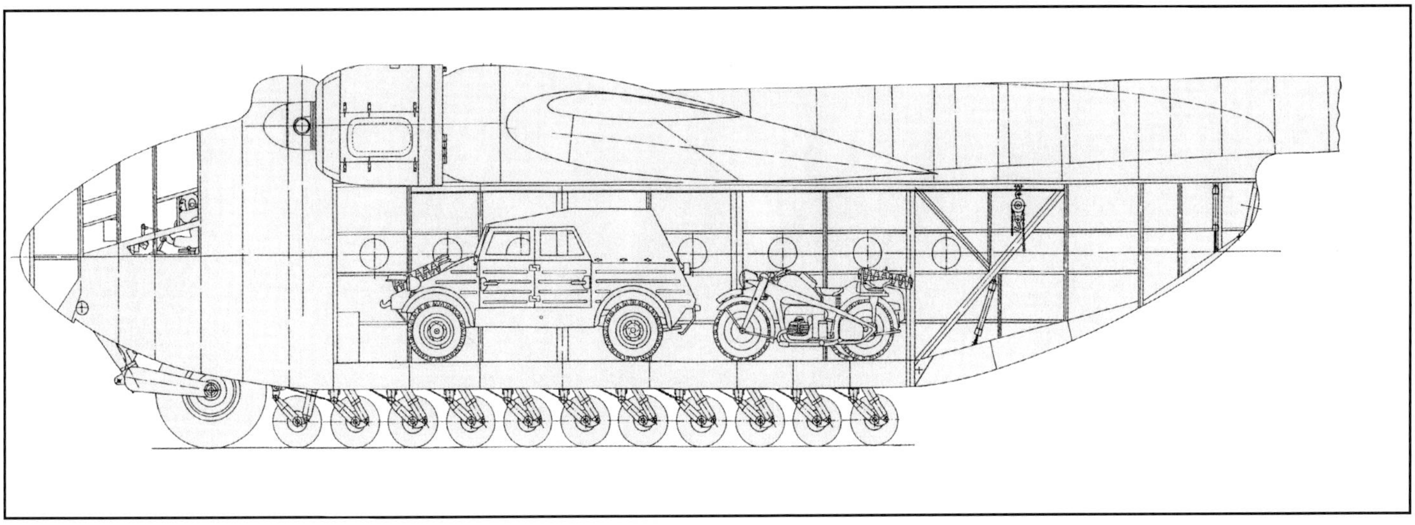

Graphic depiction of an aircraft with a typical load..

Drawing: Sengfelder

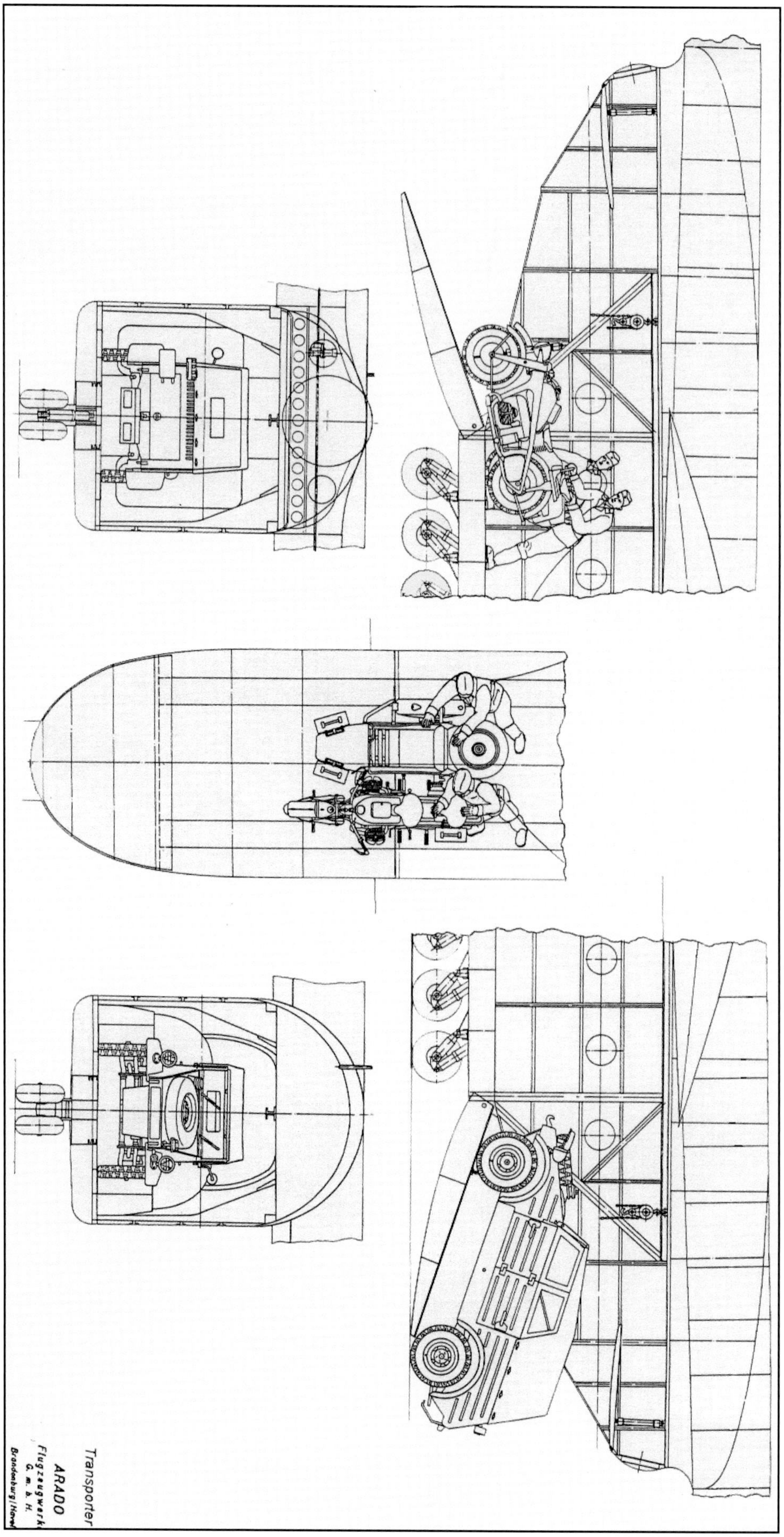

Diagram: Loading
Drawing: Sengfelder

Ar 232 V2 (Werk-Nr. 232 0002, VD+YD) during testing. Photo: DASA

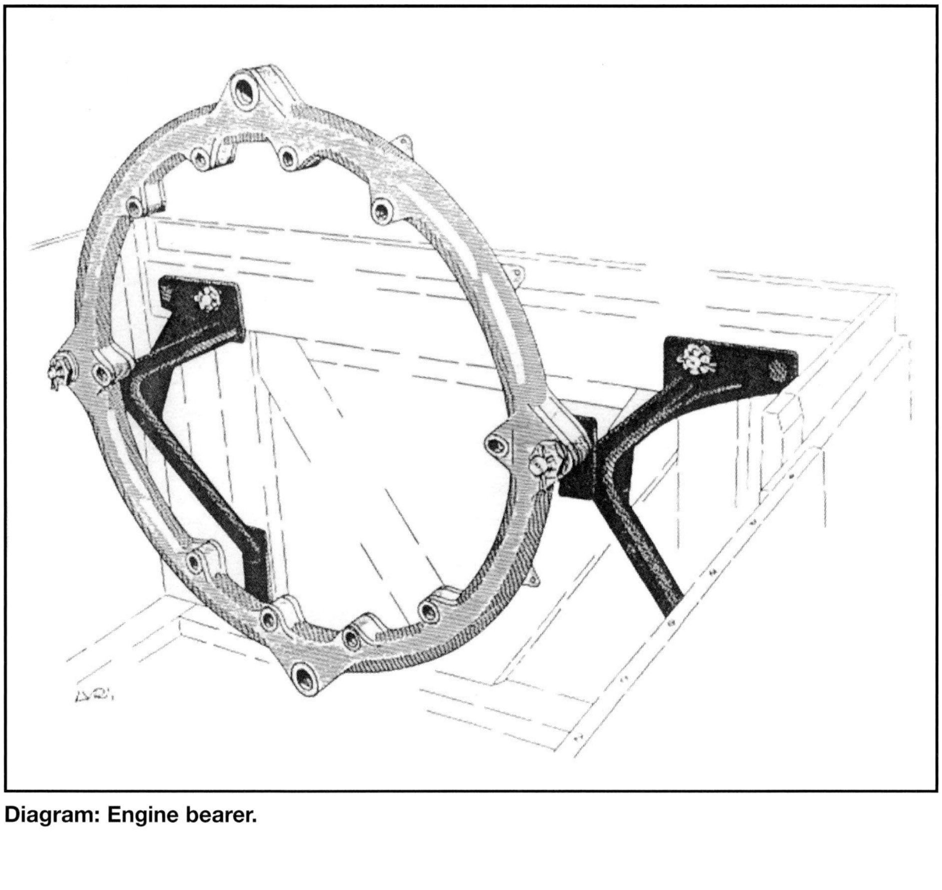

Diagram: Engine bearer.

metal, and as its only advantage compared to the Ju 352 is shorter landing and takeoff, the Generalfeldmarschall once again asked that serious consideration be given as to whether this type cannot be dropped. About four Ju 352s can be delivered for every Ar 232."

In September 1943 it was decided that only three units would be built instead of the envisaged delivery of twenty. By that time five Ar 232 B-0s were flying. Three more were in the final assembly stage in Brandenburg. Major component and single item production for the remaining twelve was under way. Against this background a delivery order for eight aircraft was initially maintained, and in the delivery plans of May and June 1944 this was increased to twelve units.

The report relating to the demonstration of an Ar 232 B-0 on 23 November 1944 contained the note: "Because of the expensive design, only a pre-production series of 20 aircraft can be built." This suggests that

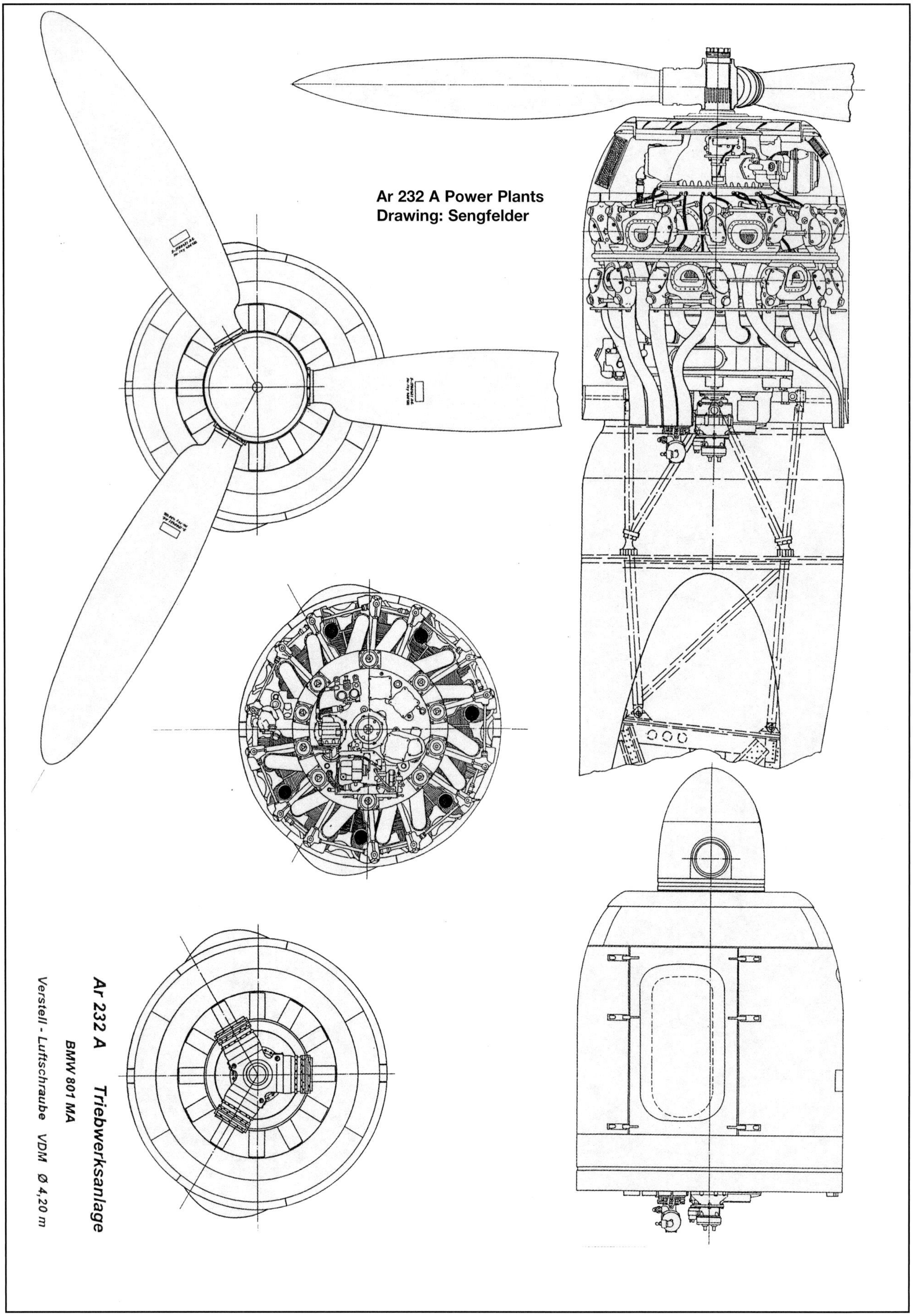

Ar 232 A Power Plants
Drawing: Sengfelder

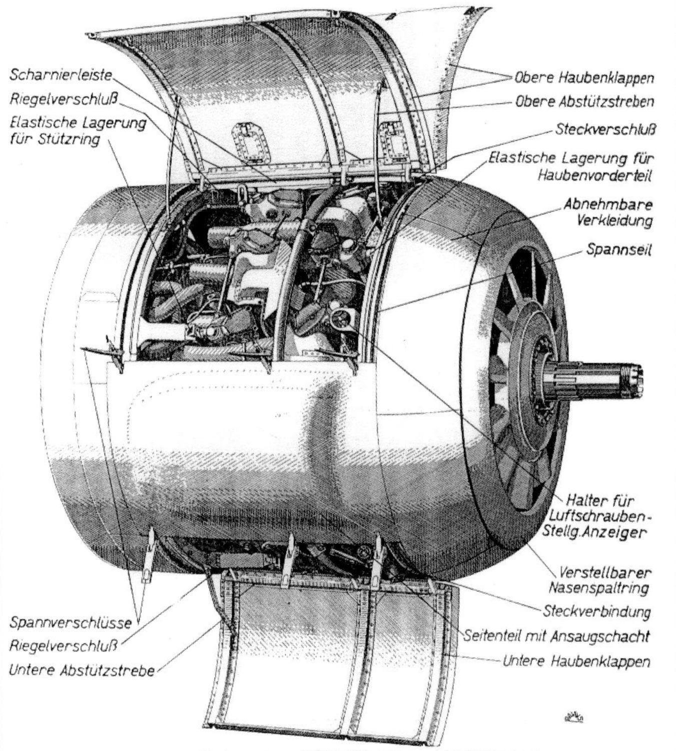

Motoranlage BMW 801 MA und BMW 801 ML mit geöffneten Haubenklappen

BMW 801 MA and BMW 801 ML power plant with open servicing panels.

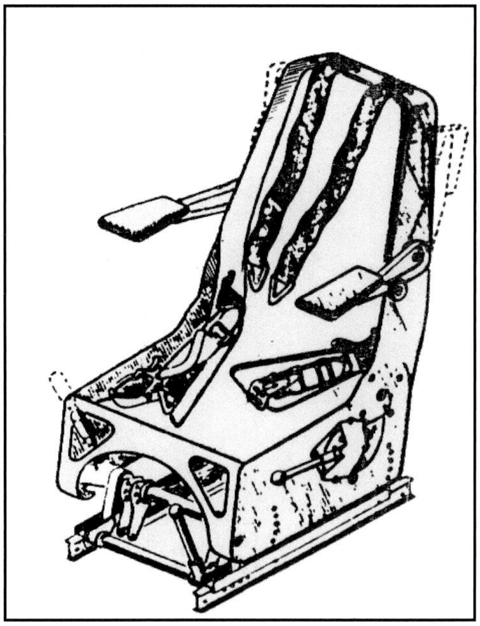

Drawing of the pilot's seat.

Forward view of the Arado Ar 232 A-0 V1.

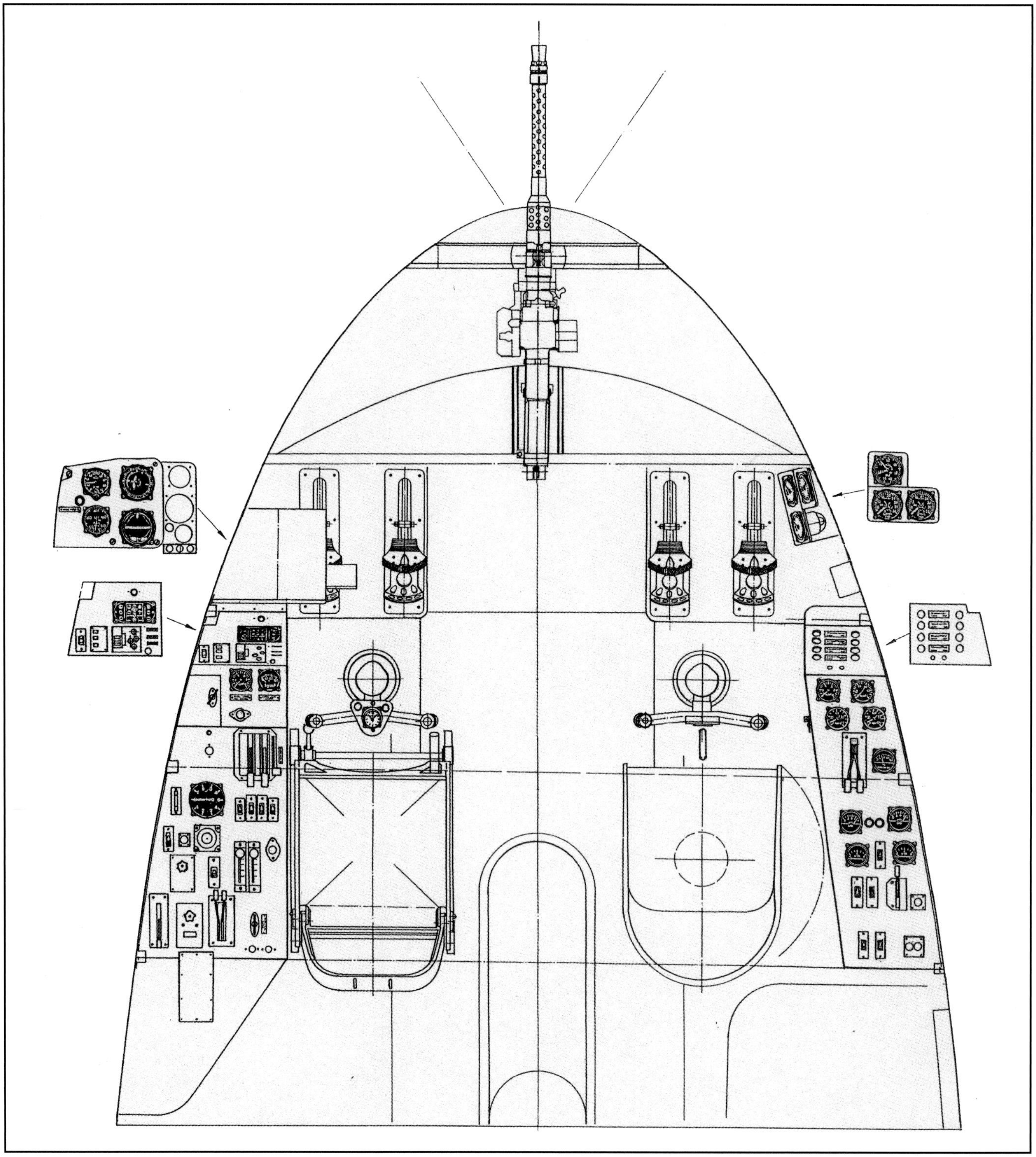

Cockpit layout.
Drawing: Sengfelder

delivery of the remaining twelve aircraft was expected. There was obvious uncertainty as to the actual state of deliveries, for an aircraft selected for a demonstration in Rechlin on 13 July 1944 was wrongly identified as the Ar 232 B-020 (Werk-Nr. 011 0032). In fact, just ten aircraft were delivered by 15 July 1944.

On 13 June 1944 Stabsingenieur Bader demonstrated the Ar 232 B-010 in Rechlin. The subsequent report contained the following information:

"The area consisted of four ditches up to 1.5 meters wide, each with a wall of loose sand approx. 180 cm high in front of and behind the ditch, with small bomb craters scattered among them. The aircraft took off and landed over these obstacles. In some cases the aircraft was set down right on a trench. Made a great impression."

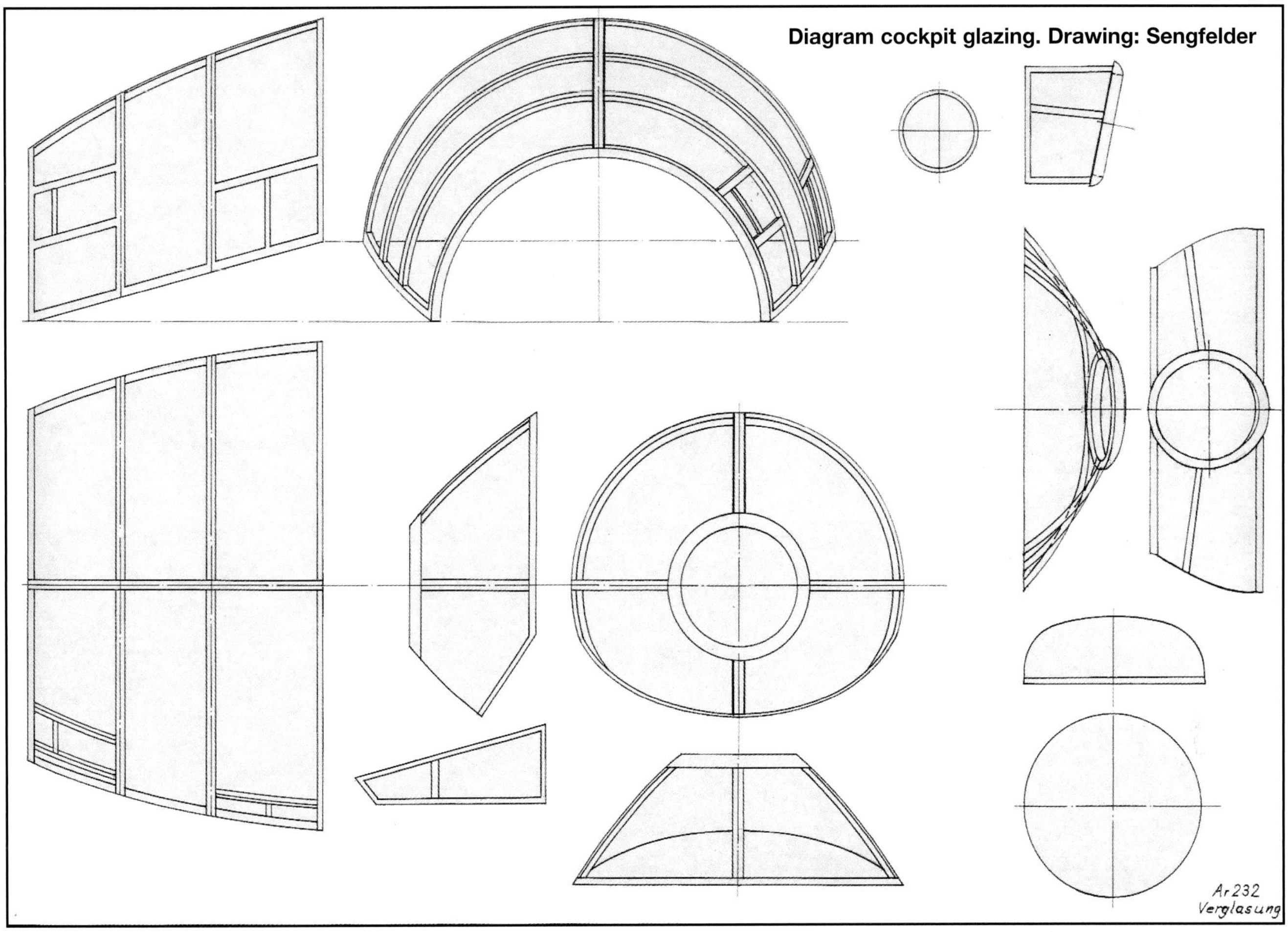

Diagram cockpit glazing. Drawing: Sengfelder

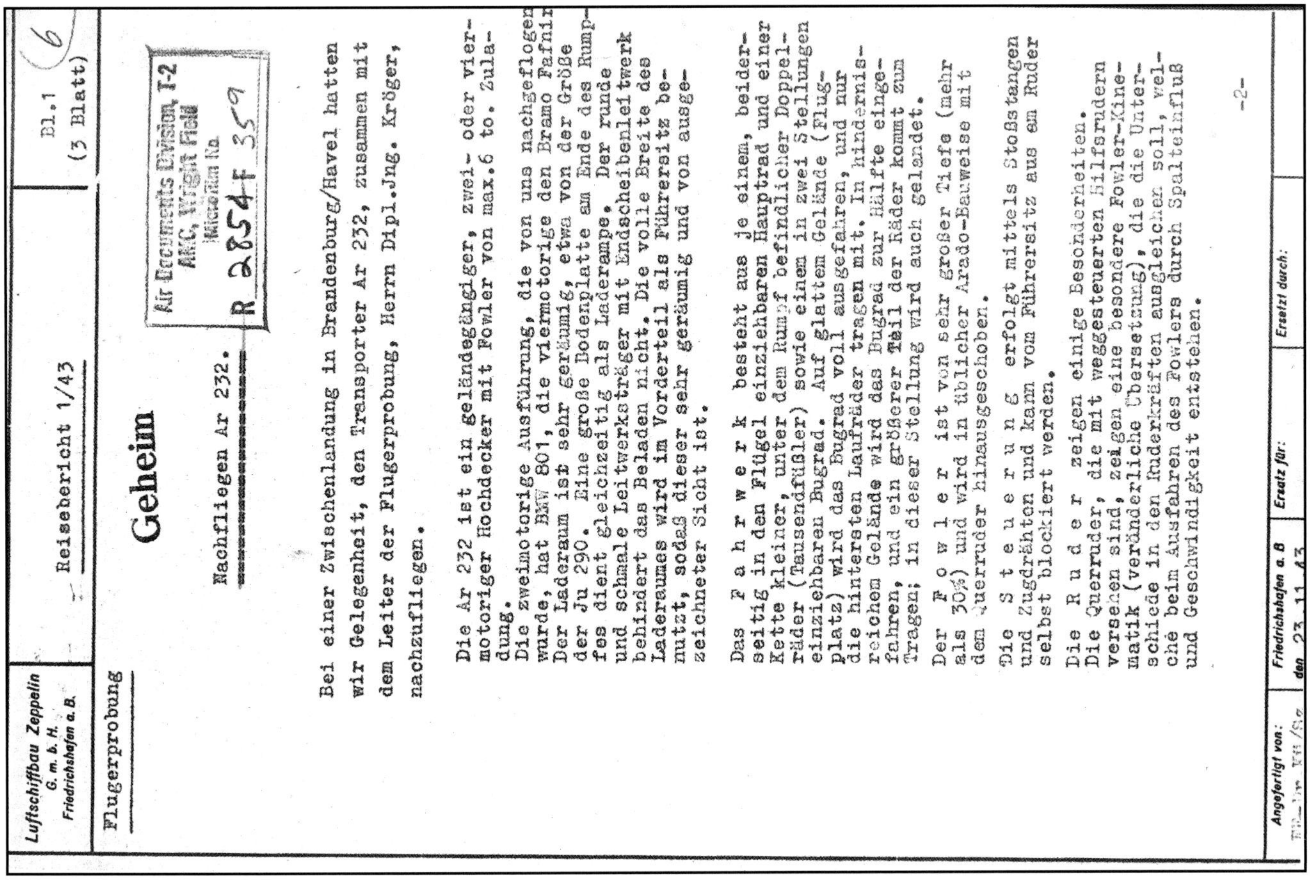

Luftschiffbau Zeppelin G. m. b. H. Friedrichshafen a. B.	Reisebericht 1/43	Bl.1 (3 Blatt) 6

Flugerprobung

Geheim

Nachfliegen Ar 232.

Bei einer Zwischenlandung in Brandenburg/Havel hatten wir Gelegenheit, den Transporter Ar 232, zusammen mit dem Leiter der Flugerprobung, Herrn Dipl.Jng. Kröger, nachzufliegen.

Die Ar 232 ist ein geländegängiger, zwei- oder viermotoriger Hochdecker mit Fowler von max.6 to. Zuladung.
Die zweimotorige Ausführung, die von uns nachgeflogen wurde, hat BMW 801, die viermotorige den Bramo Fafnir. Der Laderaum ist sehr geräumig, etwa von der Größe der Ju 290. Eine große Bodenplatte am Ende des Rumpfes dient gleichzeitig als Laderampe. Der runde und schmale Leitwerksträger mit Endscheibenleitwerk behindert das Beladen nicht. Die volle Breite des Laderaumes wird im Vorderteil als Führersitz benutzt, sodaß dieser sehr geräumig und von ausgezeichneter Sicht ist.

Das F a h r w e r k besteht aus je einem, beiderseitig in den Flügel einziehbaren Hauptrad und einer Kette kleiner, unter dem Rumpf befindlicher Doppelräder (Tausendfüßler) sowie einem in zwei Stellungen einziehbaren Bugrad. Auf glattem Gelände (Flugplatz) wird das Bugrad voll ausgefahren, und nur die hintersten Laufräder tragen mit. In hindernisreichem Gelände wird das Bugrad zur Hälfte eingefahren, und ein größerer Teil der Räder kommt zum Tragen; in dieser Stellung wird auch gelandet.

Der F o w l e r ist von sehr großer Tiefe (mehr als 30%) und wird in üblicher Arado-Bauweise mit dem Querruder hinausgeschoben.

Die S t e u e r u n g erfolgt mittels Stoßstangen und Zugdrähten und kann vom Führersitz aus am Ruder selbst blockiert werden.

Die R u d e r zeigen einige Besonderheiten.
Die Querruder, die mit weggesteuerten Hilfsrudern versehen sind, zeigen eine besondere Fowler-Kinematik (veränderliche Übersetzung), die die Unterschiede in den Ruderkräften ausgleichen soll, welche beim Ausfahren des Fowlers durch Spalteinfluß und Geschwindigkeit entstehen.

-2-

Angefertigt von:	Friedrichshafen a. B	Ersatz für:	Ersetzt durch:
FK-Ltr. Kü/Sg	den 23.11.43		

Im Seitenruder zeigt das Hilfsruder ein Langloch mit Federzentrierung, das dazu dienen soll, den (weggesteuerten) Hilfsruderausschlag erst von einem bestimmten Seitenruderausschlag an eintreten zu lassen, um die Ruderkräfte um die Nullage herum hochzuhalten.
Das Höhenruder zeigt keine Besonderheiten.

Der Schwerpunktbereich liegt bei 23 - 30 %, der Indifferenzpunkt bei etwa 32 %.

Das Nachfliegen hatte folgendes Ergebnis :

Sehr angenehmes und wendiges Rollen, das nach Auskunft von Herrn Bader (E-Stelle Rechlin) auch das Überrollen sehr breiter und tiefer Gräben und ca.60 cm hoher Röhren gestattet. Die Geländegängigkeit soll auch bei Landungen in einem Grabenfeld (von je 2 m Grabenbreite) überzeugend bewiesen worden sein.

Die Sicht ist ausgezeichnet, das nach Art eines Motorradlenkers ausgeführte Handrad weniger angenehm.

Der Start war überraschend kurz. Mit ausgefahrenem Fowler stieg das Flugzeug mit 100 km/h Geschwindigkeit in gut steuerbaren Zustand weg. Nach Einfahren der Fowler ging die Geschwindigkeit über 200 km/h

Die Reiseflug - Geschwindigkeit lag nahe bei 300 km/h. Wendigkeit sehr befriedigend.

Ruderkräfte und -wirkungen:

Im Seiten- und Höhenruder ist eine ständige Unruhe zu bemerken. Die Höhenruderkräfte sind im Reiseflug etwas hoch, ebenso die Querruderkräfte; die Seitenruderkräfte sind befriedigend.
Die Wirkungen aller Ruder sind - jedenfalls im eingefowlerten Zustand - gut. Kraftverlauf einwandfrei, Rückführung gut.

Längsstabilität befriedigend (gute Austrimmbarkeit);
Seitenstabilität jetzt sehr gut. Dieser Punkt hatte in der Entwicklung größere Schwierigkeiten bereitet. Um die Richtungsstabilität nicht zu sehr zu verkleinern, wurden die Schieberollmomente durch höhere V-Form vergrößert. V-Form jetzt = 6° (wie Me 323). Kurvensteuerbarkeit allein mit Seitenruder sehr befriedigend; keinerlei Neigung mehr zum Spiralsturz. Die Gierschwingungen sind gut gedämpft (nach 1/2 Periode); die Querrudergiermomente sind genügend klein.

-3-

Angefertigt von:	Friedrichshafen a. B	Ersatz für:	Ersetzt durch:

Luftschiffbau Zeppelin G. m. b. H. Friedrichshafen a. B.	Reisebericht 1/43	Bl.3

Motorausfall läßt sich ohne viel Kräfteaufwand mit Seitenruder halten und ergibt keine größere Lastigkeitsänderung. Auffallend ist, daß das Ausfahren der Ladeluke nach unten im Fluge (Abwurf) kein kopflastiges, sondern ein schwanzlastiges Moment ergibt (Abwindverstärkung am Leitwerk).

Die Landung ging mit ausgefahrenem Fowler in sehr steilem Gleitwinkel bei 100 km/h Anschwebegeschwindigkeit vor sich. Die Ausrollstrecke betrug nur 120 m.

Im ganzen machte das Flugzeug einen sehr günstigen Eindruck; wegen der kostspieligen Bauart kann aber nur eine Nullserie von 20 Stück gebaut werden.

Friedrichshafen, den 23.11.43
FE Dr.Kü/Sz

Küttner ....   Starbati ....
Erprobungsleiter   Flugbetriebsleiter

Verteiler:
Hr.Dir.Eckener
Stender
Fröhlich
Foerster
Nothelfer
Schmid
Molt
Dr.Küttner
Starbati
Krämer
zdA. Fremde Fl.Muster.2x

Angefertigt von:	Friedrichshafen a. B	Ersatz für:	Ersetzt durch:
FE-Dr.Kü/Sz	den 23.11.43		

Pilot's control column.

Starboard control column.

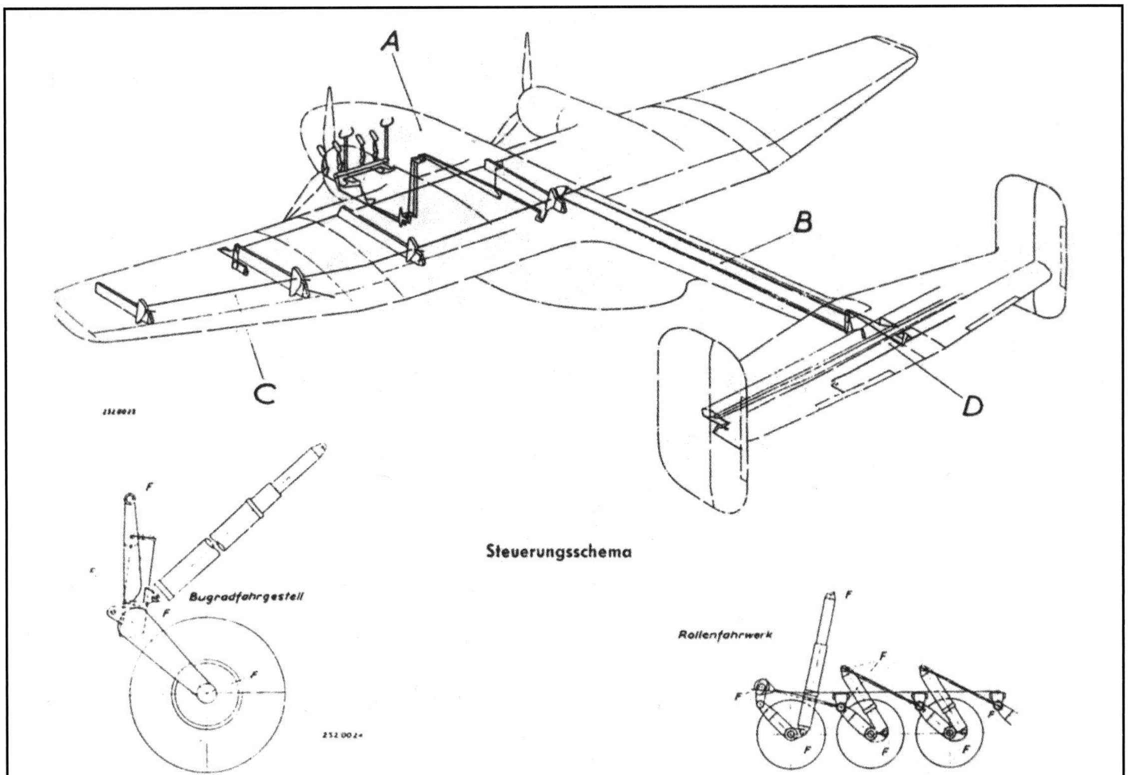

Undercarriage and control system of the Ar 232 A-0.

Source: Ar 232 A-0 handbook.

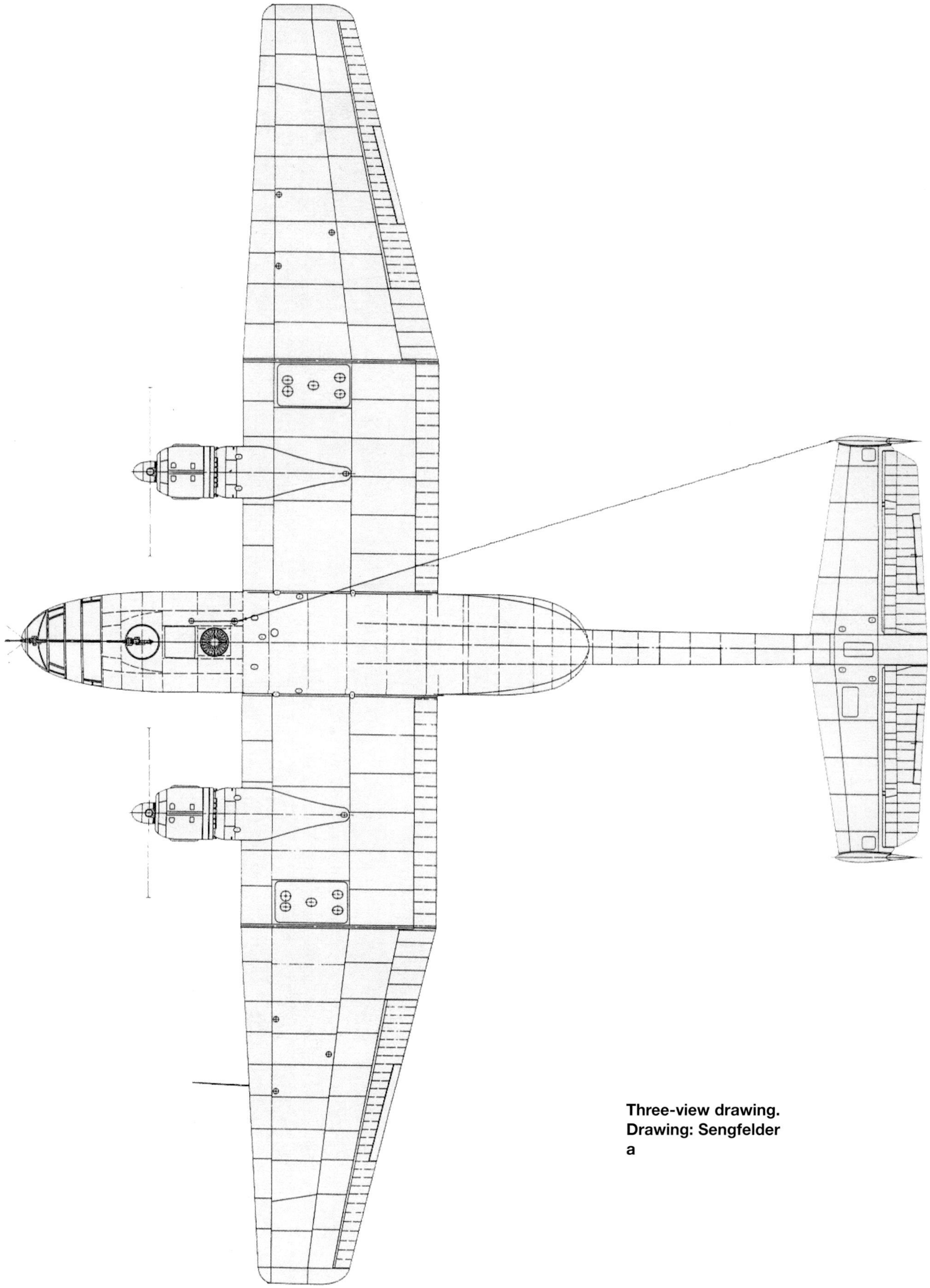

Three-view drawing.
Drawing: Sengfelder
a

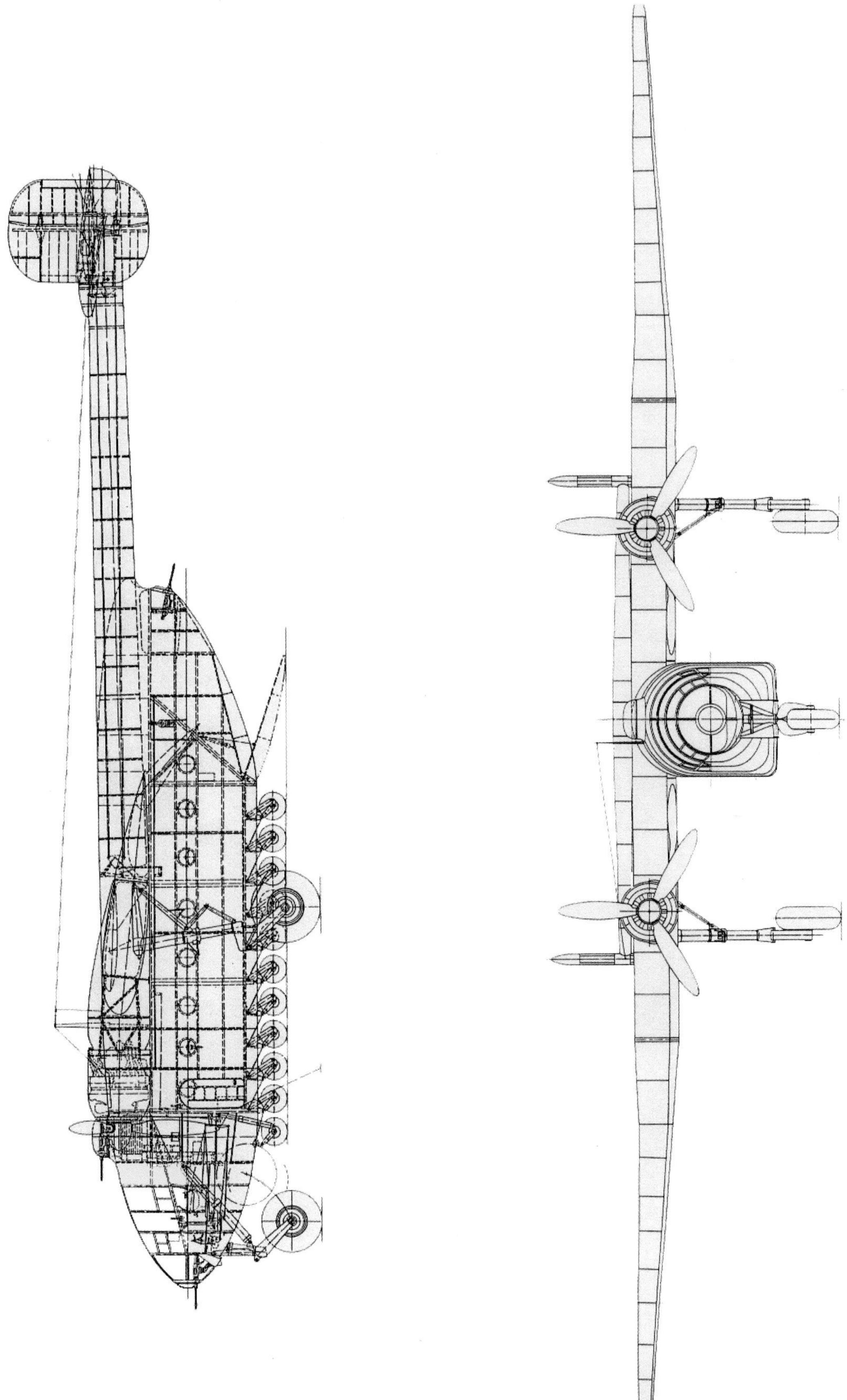

Rear view of the Arado Ar 232 A-0 in Orel in the winter of 1943-44 illustrated on Page 4. **Photo: Klein Archive**

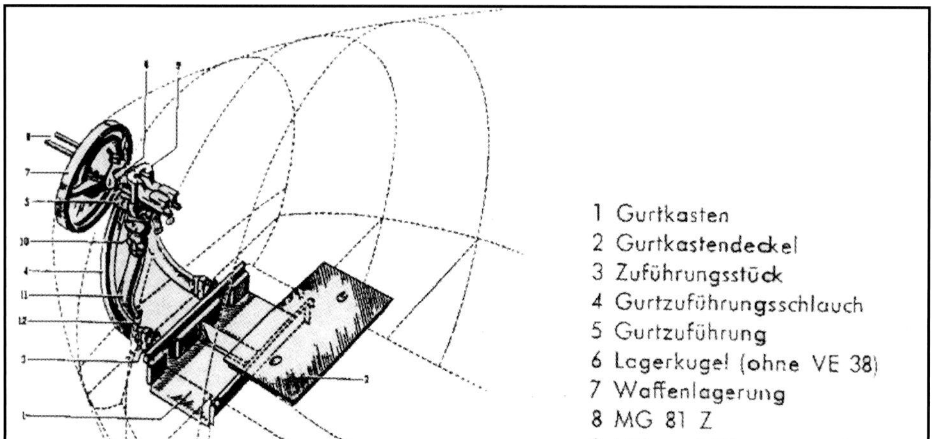

Nose gun position (A-Stand) of the Arado Ar 232.v

Though the Ar 232 had demonstrated its capabilities once again, some technicians at Rechlin like Heinrich Beauvais remained skeptical. They were convinced that they "heard all sorts of noises from inside the aircraft" when it ran over the ditches and "couldn't help thinking that the heavy jolts while taxiing had caused damage". On 23 November 1944 in Brandenburg, however, the Ar 232 B-0 made "a very favorable impression" on representatives of the Luftschiffbau Zeppelin GmbH, which had been tasked with further development of the Messerschmitt Me 323 transport. Control effectiveness and stability were found to be good. In their opinion view from the cockpit was "excellent", the takeoff "surprisingly short". They also observed that with Fowler flaps extended "the aircraft climbed away at 100 kph in a well controlled state". Landing with Fowler flaps extended was made at a very steep glide angle at an approach speed of 100 kph. Rollout after landing was just 120 meters.

After the production of transport aircraft was halted on 28 June 1944 because of the critical military situation and planned development of the simplified Ar 432 transport also had to be abandoned, production of the Ar 232 ended on 30 November with delivery of the Ar 232 B-011 pre-production aircraft.

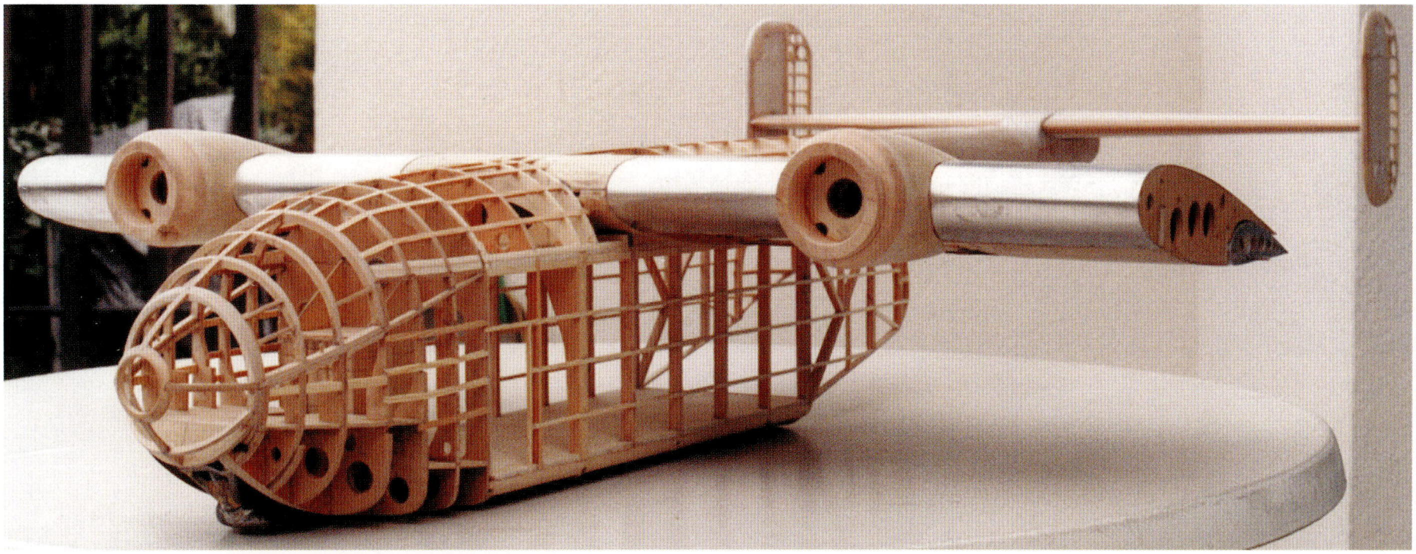

Günter Sengfelder's Ar 232 model in the initial stages.

Model after skinning.

Close-up with working flap system.

The huge model in Günter Sengfelder's private museum.

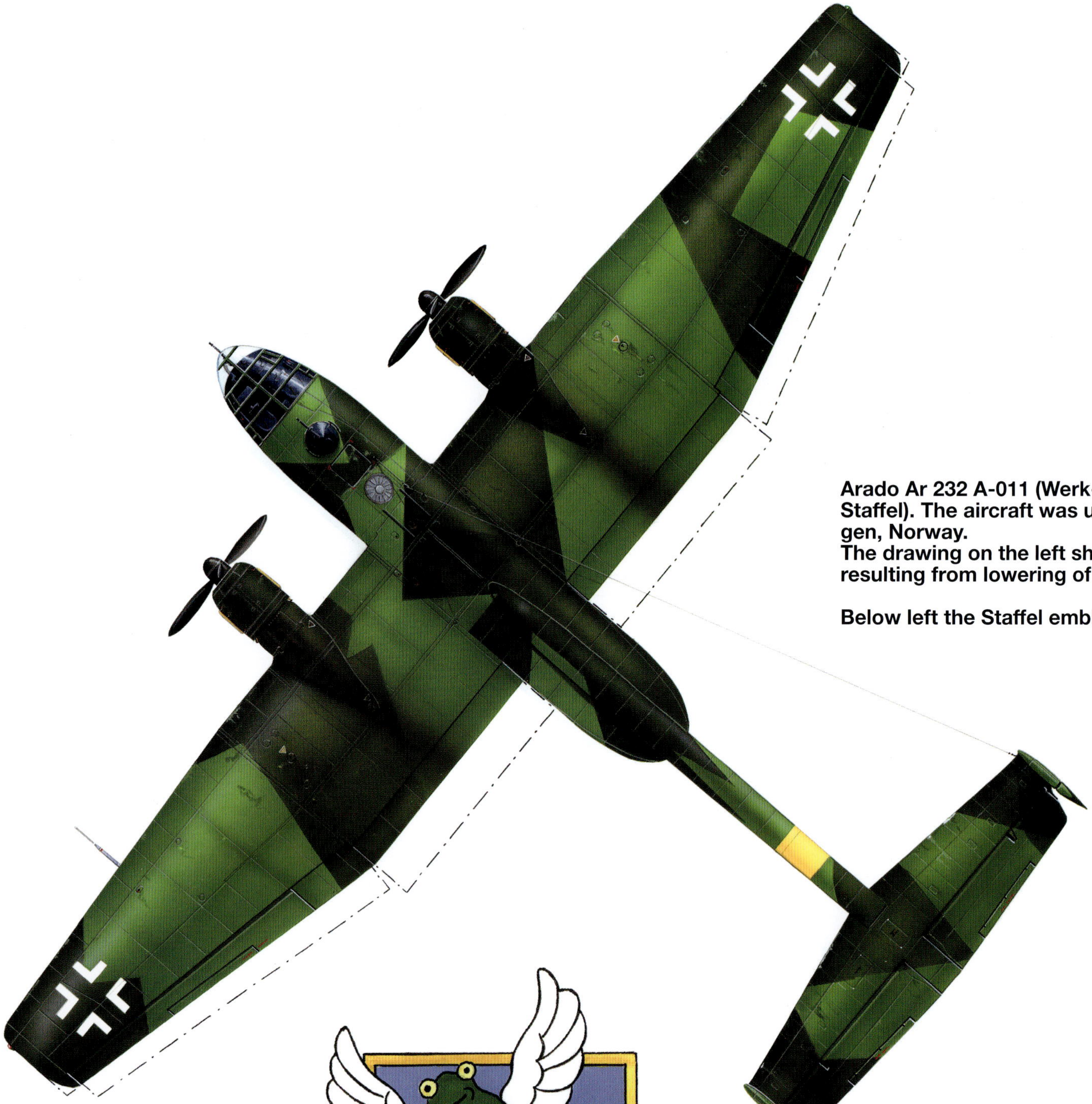

Arado Ar 232 A-011 (Werk-Nr. 01
Staffel). The aircraft was used a
gen, Norway.
The drawing on the left shows ir
resulting from lowering of the fl

Below left the Staffel emblem of

The model's undercarriage in the retracted position.

Main undercarriage extended.

The extremely detailed model cockpit.

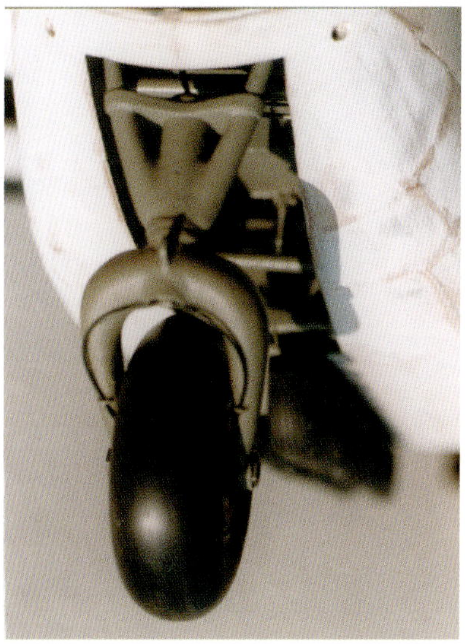

The sturdy nosewheel gear.

Aft gun position (C-Stand) of the Ar 232.

The huge increase in wing area with the landing flaps extended is readily apparent in this view of the model.

Rear view of Günter Sengfelder's model with landing flaps extended.

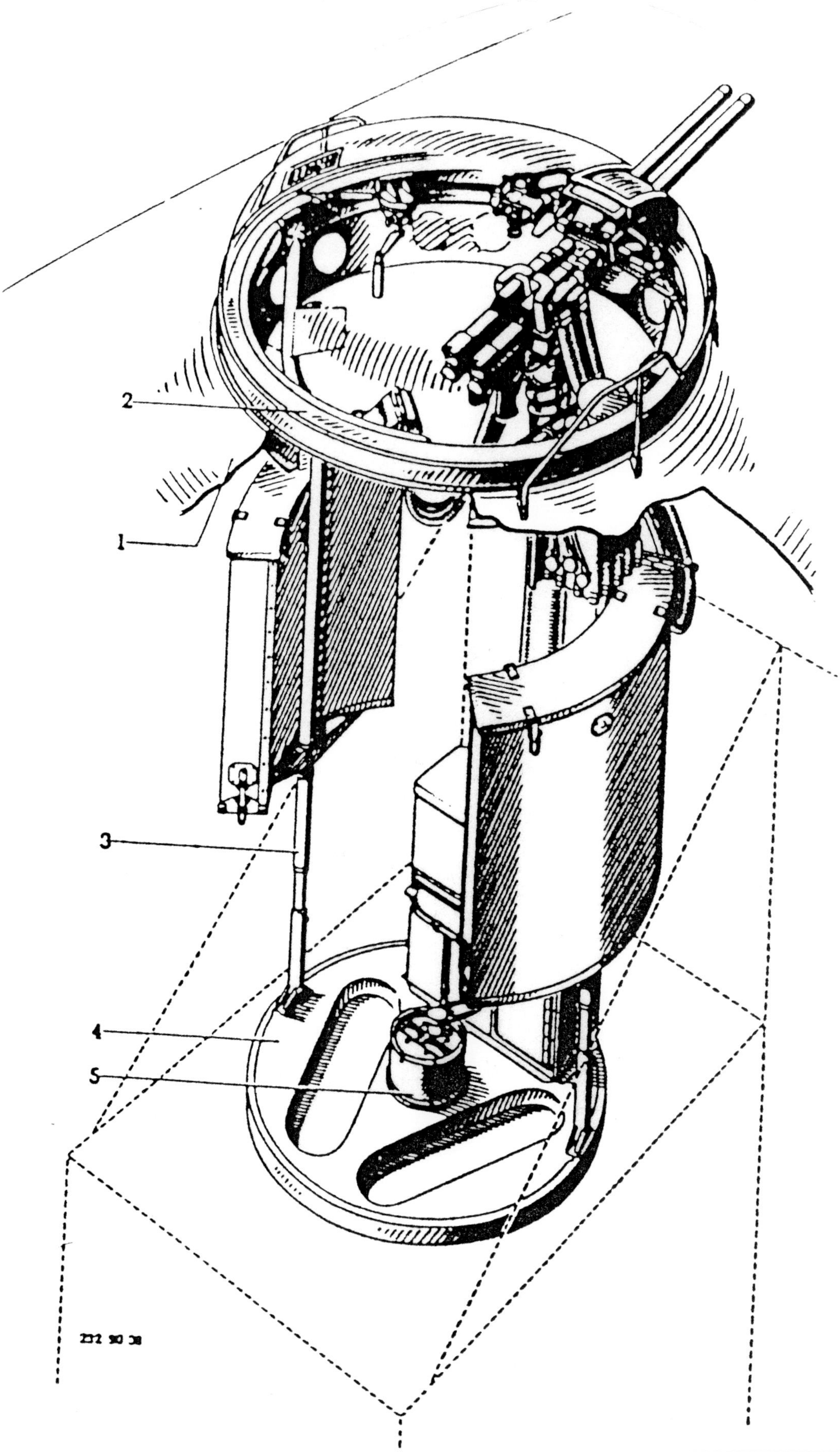

A drawing of the Arado Ar 232's dorsal turret.

View from above of the Arado Ar 232 A-0 V1.

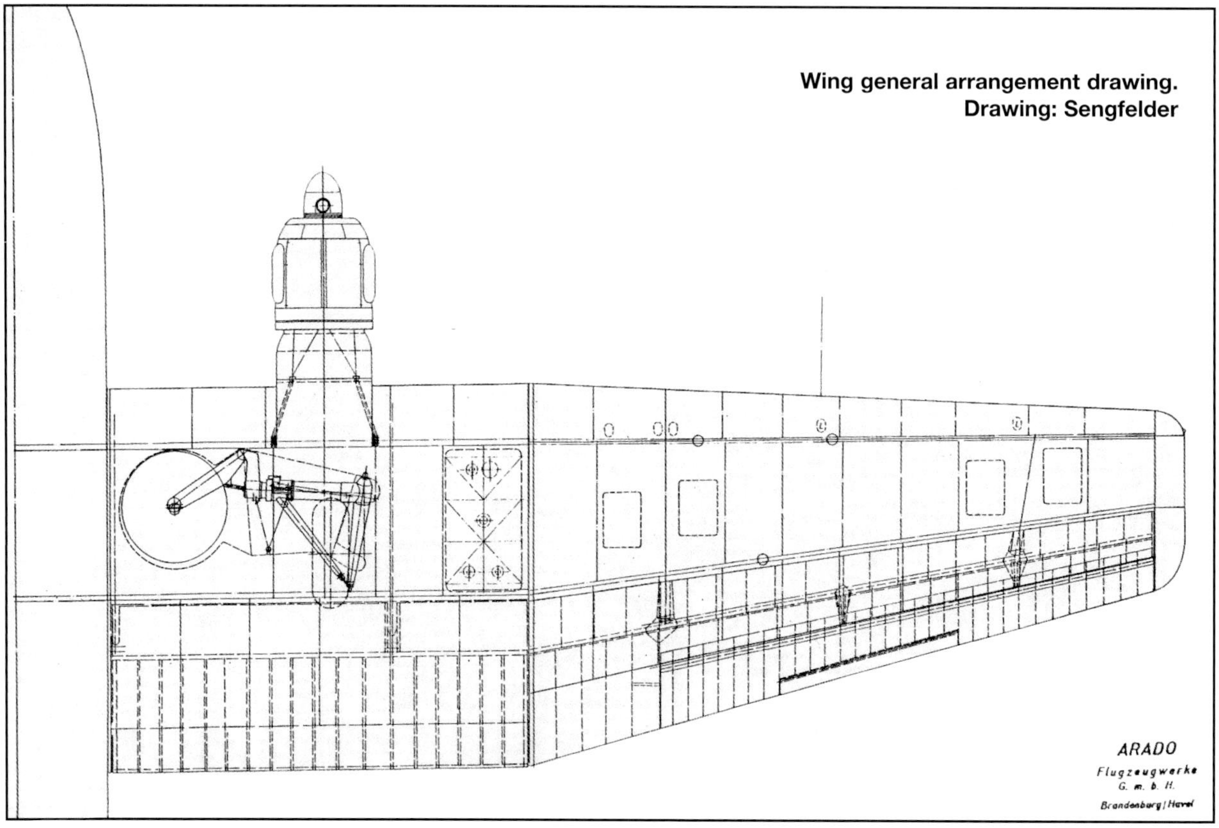

Wing general arrangement drawing.
Drawing: Sengfelder

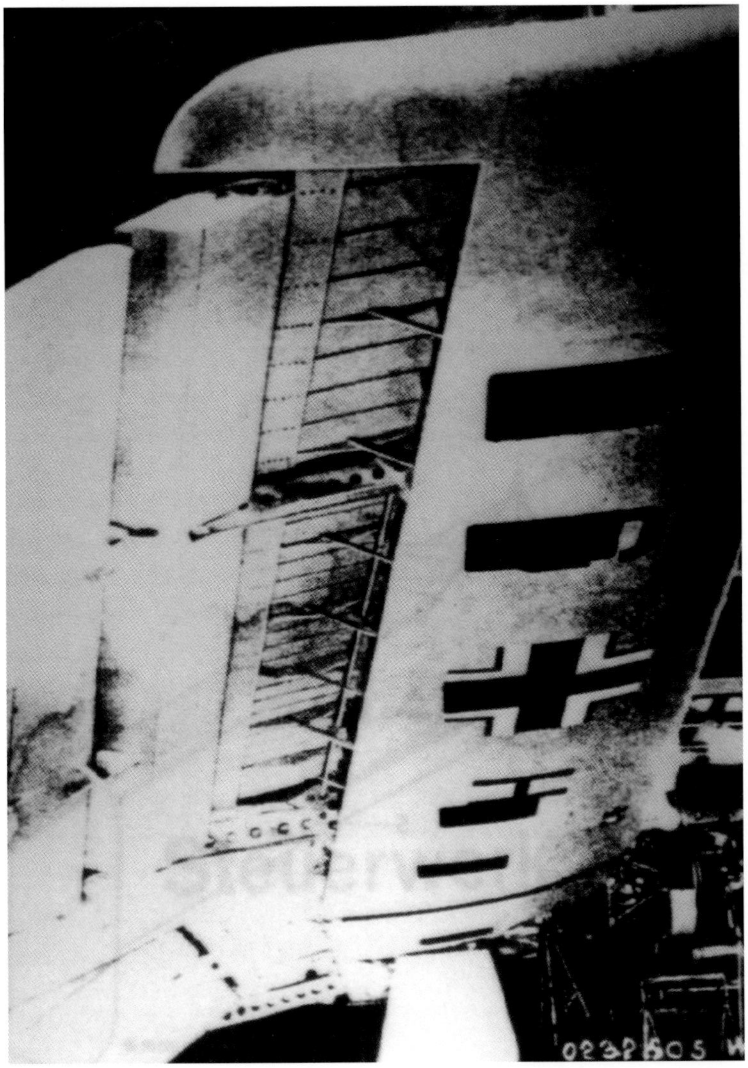

Landing flap of the Ar 232 V1. Source: Ar 232 A-0 handbook.

Arado retained the Ar 232 V2 as a test-bed until the end of the war. It also used the Ar 232 A-05 (Werk-Nr. 010 0007, VD+YE), which had been test flown by Walter Kröger on 22 April 1943, as a company transport, including in trials of the Ar 234 jet bomber. On 10 June 1944 company pilot Jakob Kunz landed at Hirschberg airport, probably in the Ar 232 A-05, which had been test-flown by Rechlin pilots in the summer of 1943. In agreement with Walter Kröger, Hans Rebeski had received permission to demonstrate the aircraft to members of the design bureau, which he headed and which had been relocated to Landeshut, Silesia, as part of a "company outing". There was an unexpected incident when the local Volkssturm, suspecting that the aircraft was dropping off enemy spies, tried to prevent the aircraft from taking off again.

The Ar 232 was mainly used to supply encircled areas of the front on the Eastern Front and in the rough terrain of the Arctic Front. The first and only unit equipped solely with the Ar 232 was the 7. Staffel of the Ergänzungs-Transportgeschwader (replacement transport wing), which was formed in Berlin-Schönwalde in June 1943 and transferred to Eger in December. The unit never had more than eight aircraft at any one time, as was the case in the spring and summer of 1944.

According to design chief Hans Rebeski, the Ar 232 A-01 (Werk-Nr. 010 0003, VD+YA), which was completed in November 1942, was supposed to have been used for a short time to evacuate wounded from the Stalingrad area. The aircraft did not leave until after Stalingrad had fallen on 6 February 1943, however. Rebeski had doubts about turning

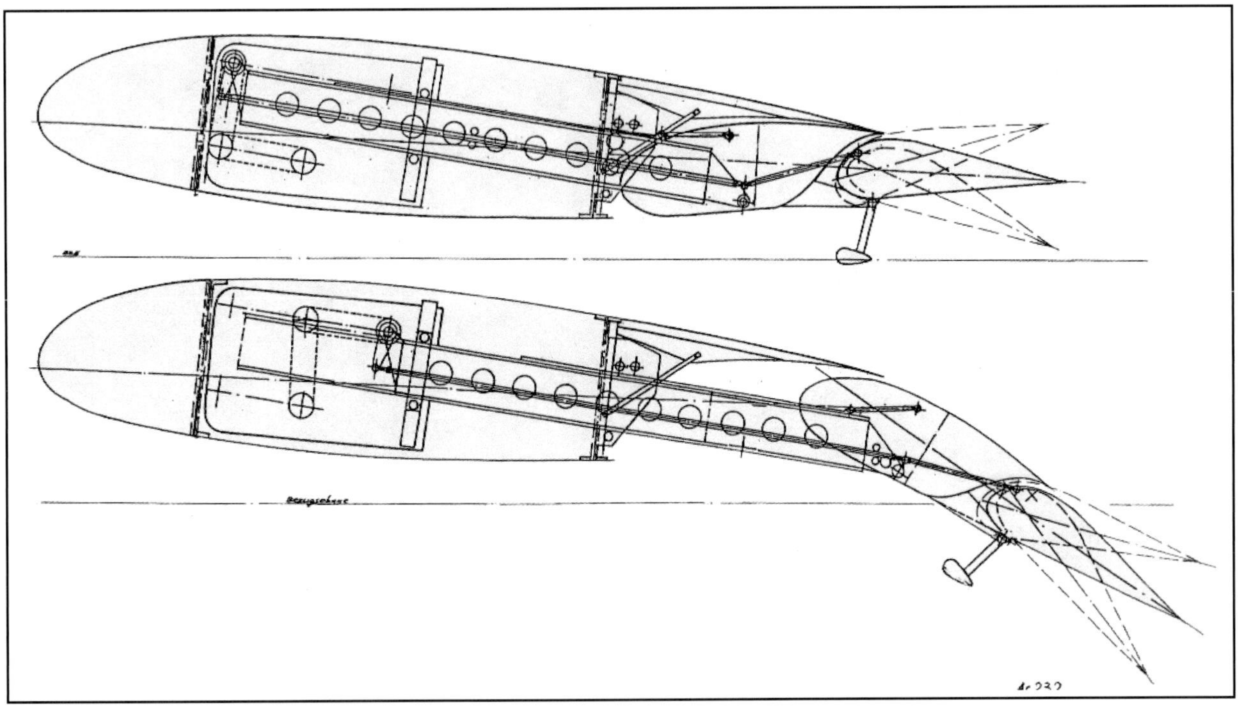

General arrangement drawing showing the aileron linkage and system. Drawing: Sengfelder

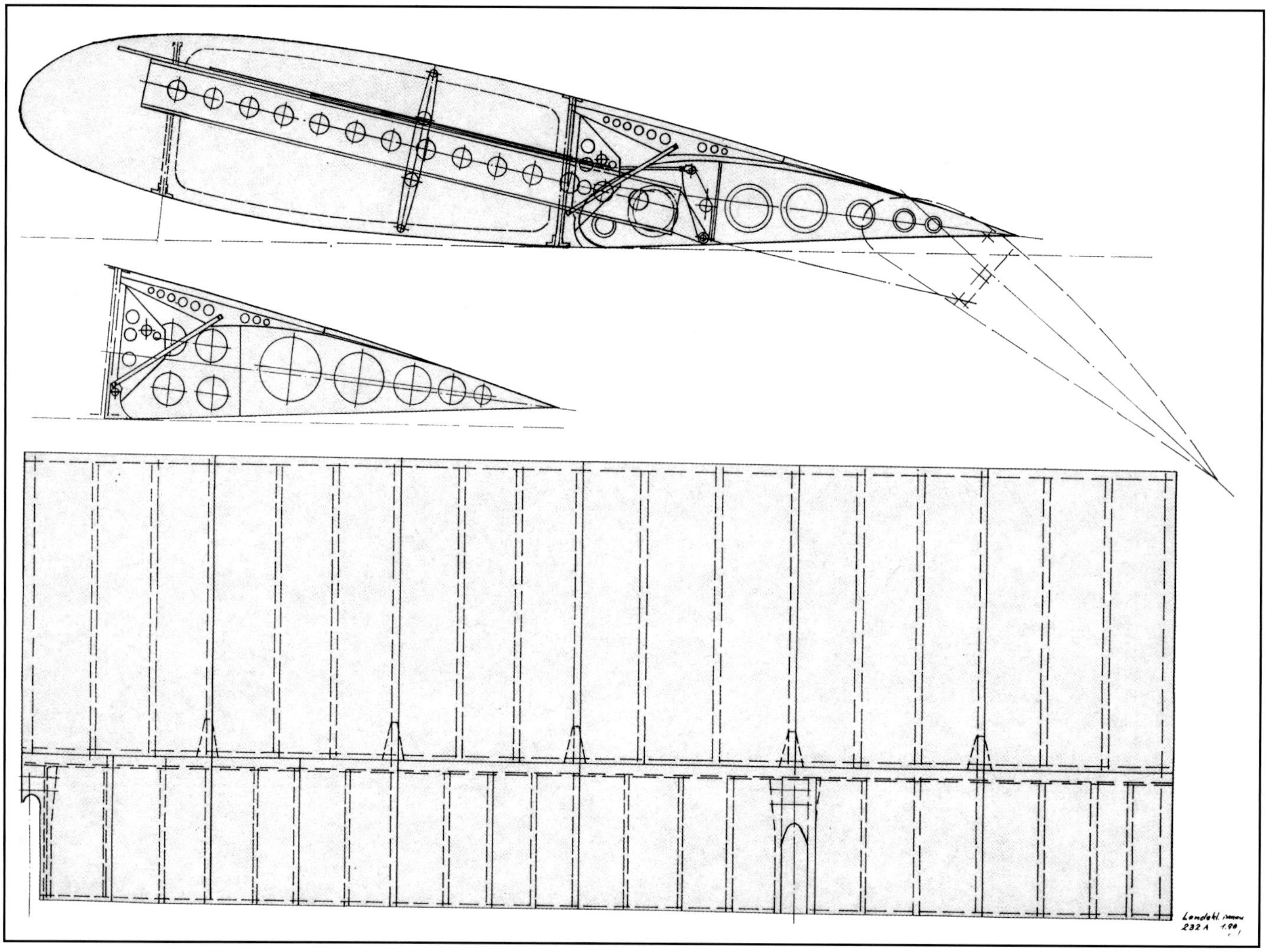

General arrangement drawing of the landing flap. **Drawing: Sengfelder**

an unproven aircraft over to a front-line unit, and in discussions with Walter Blume and the Luftwaffe command he offered to accompany the crews, taking along special tools. A traffic accident prevented him from immediately implementing his plan and the first aircraft flew ahead without him. When its inexperienced pilot descended over a wooded area near Beutnitz in an attempt to gain visual contact with the surface, the aircraft contacted the ground and crashed. Plans to use the Ar 232 A-02 (Werk-Nr. 010 0004, VD+YB), which was delivered in February 1943, for the same mission were subsequently cancelled.

On the Eastern Front the Ar 232 was mainly employed in the Odessa area and in the Crimea. The extraordinary rough field capability of the Ar 232 also proved itself in the far north of Europe. On 17 July 1943 Oblt. Rudolf Schütze took off from Brandenburg in the twin-engined Ar 232 A-010 (Werk-Nr. 010 0012, TC+EG) for Banak, Norway, the northernmost airfield in Europe. Operating with Westa 5 (Weather Staffel 5), Schütze was supposed to land in the deep snow on Spitzbergen and drop off automatic weather stations. The necessary range for these flights was achieved by installing additional fuel tanks with a capacity of 5000 liters. On landing on Spitzbergen's south cape on 24 July 1943, the right side of the main undercarriage folded. The aircraft rolled out on the multi-wheel undercarriage and then came to rest on its right wingtip. Thanks to the ability to adjust the height of the undercarriage, the crew was able to right the aircraft without assistance. The same thing happened on 7 August when the aircraft sank up to its axles in soft ground during a landing on Bear Island. During the recovery work, which lasted several days, supplies were air-dropped to the crew.

The aircraft was lost before its mission was completed as a result of a series of unfortunate circumstances. On 26 August 1943 it was supposed to be flown back to Brandenburg for overhaul and replaced by a four-engined aircraft. Radio contact was lost shortly after takeoff and the aircraft crashed and burned. The crew and all the passengers, including a number of specialists from the manufacturer, lost their lives. An investigation revealed that the right engine had failed shortly after takeoff when the aircraft was still in cloud. The only possible emergency landing sites were to the right, and the pilot was forced to turn into the dead engine. This maneuver, which is in itself difficult, was made more difficult by the poor single-engine performance of the Ar 232 A. The aircraft lost more height than expected and when it emerged from cloud it was already lower than the surrounding, approximately 150-meter high hills. When the pilots attempted to climb over one of the hills, the aircraft stalled and crashed just below the top.

The aircraft's rough field capability made it appear ideal for use in secret sabotage missions by KG 200, a special operations unit. One such operation, codenamed "Zeppelin", had as its goal the assassination of Stalin. The Soviet dictator was supposed to be killed in the Kremlin on the 27th anniversary of the October Revolution by a radio-detonated bomb concealed in a briefcase. The operation was supposed to be carried out by a Russian officer deserter, who was provided with papers identifying him as the deputy leader of the defense battalion of the 39th Soviet Army. He was accompanied by a Russian female radio operator masquerading as a sub-lieutenant in the medical service.

The first attempt to carry out the operation with the Ar 232 A-08 (Werk-Nr. 010 0010,

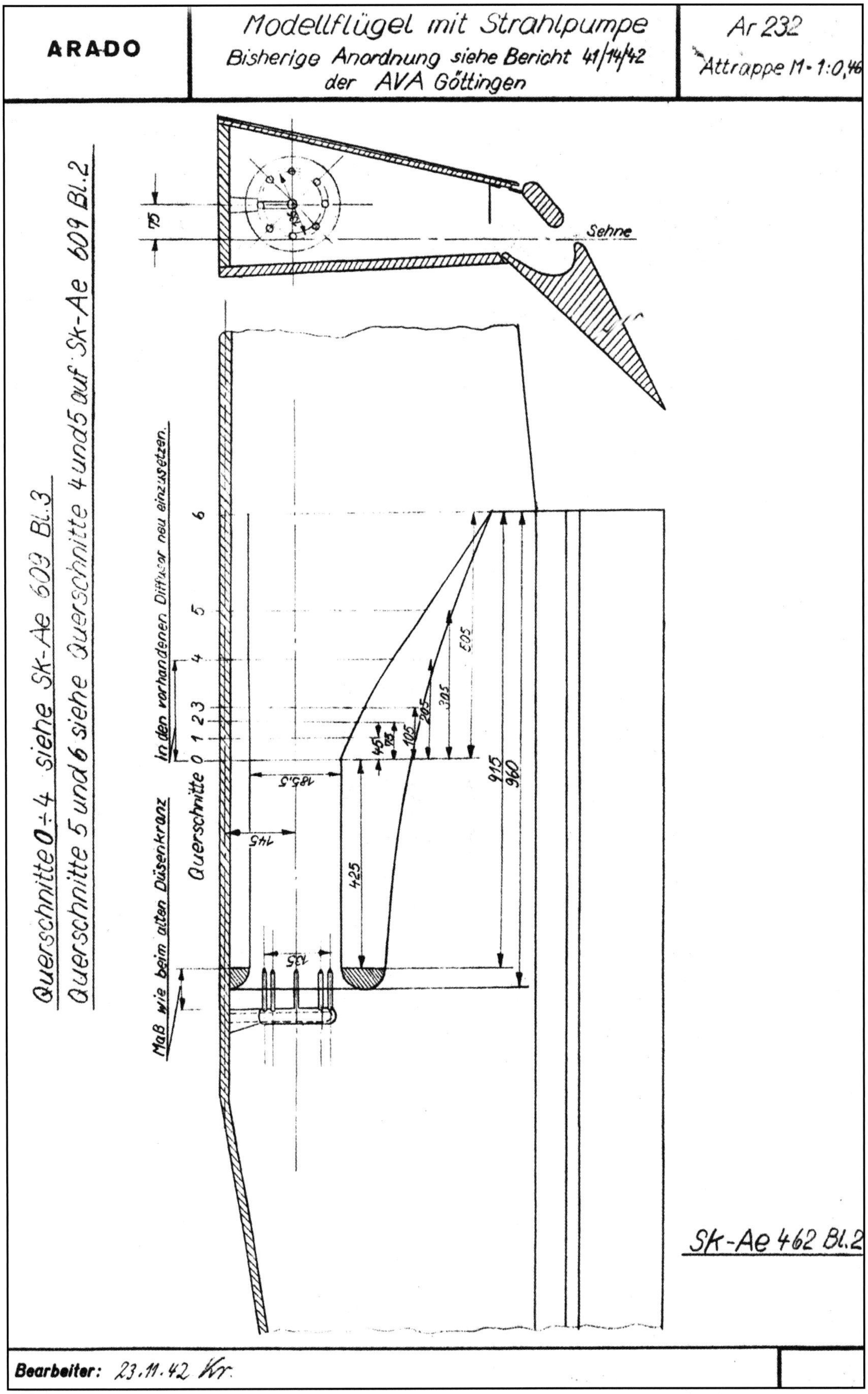

Cross-section of the jet pump for the model wing of the Ar 232 V2 for the purpose of boundary layer control.

Günter Sengfelder Archive

Arado Ar 232 A-0 V1 in June 1942 with main undercarriage lowered and no fairings on the main undercarriage legs.

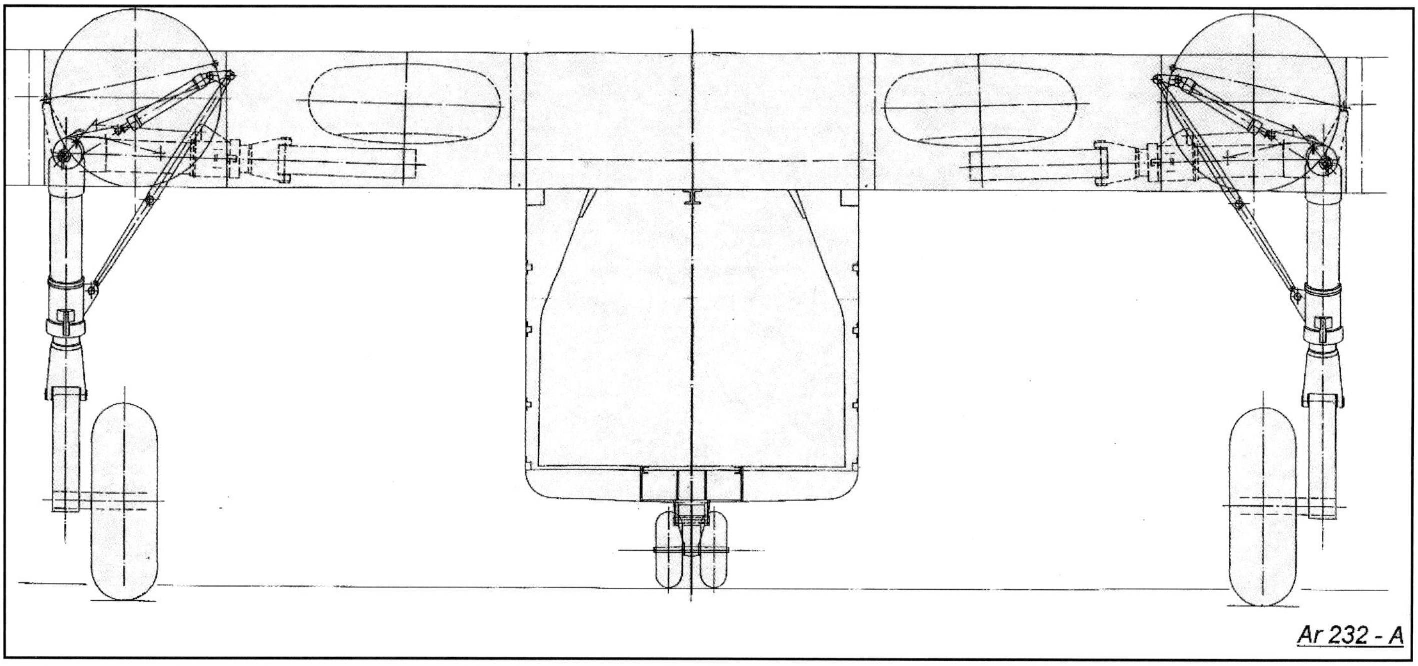

General arrangement drawing of the undercarriage. **Drawing: Sengfelder**

An Arado Ar 232 A-0 taking off from a paved runway.

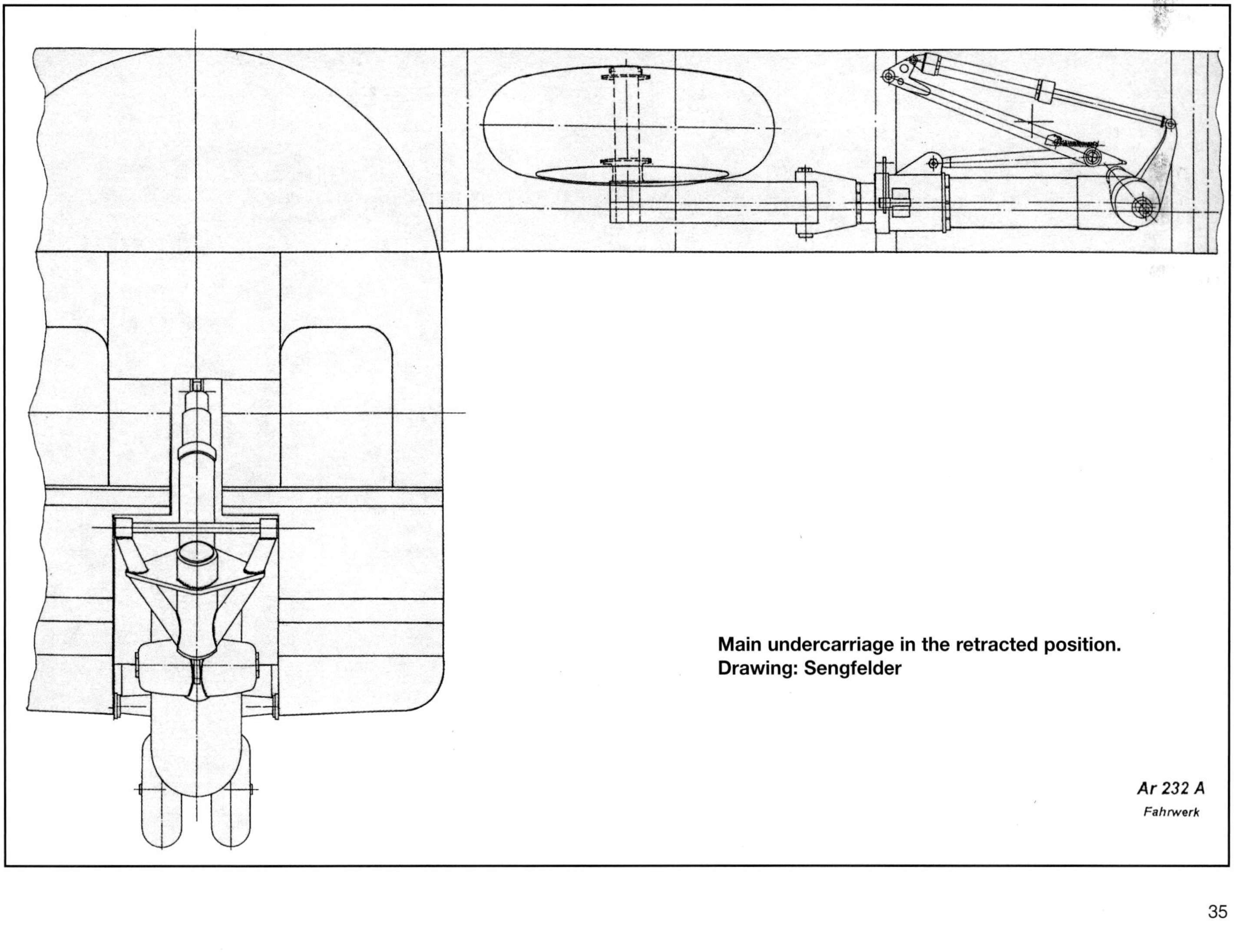

Main undercarriage in the retracted position.
Drawing: Sengfelder

Arado Ar 232 A-01, VD+YA.
It was the first A-series production aircraft.

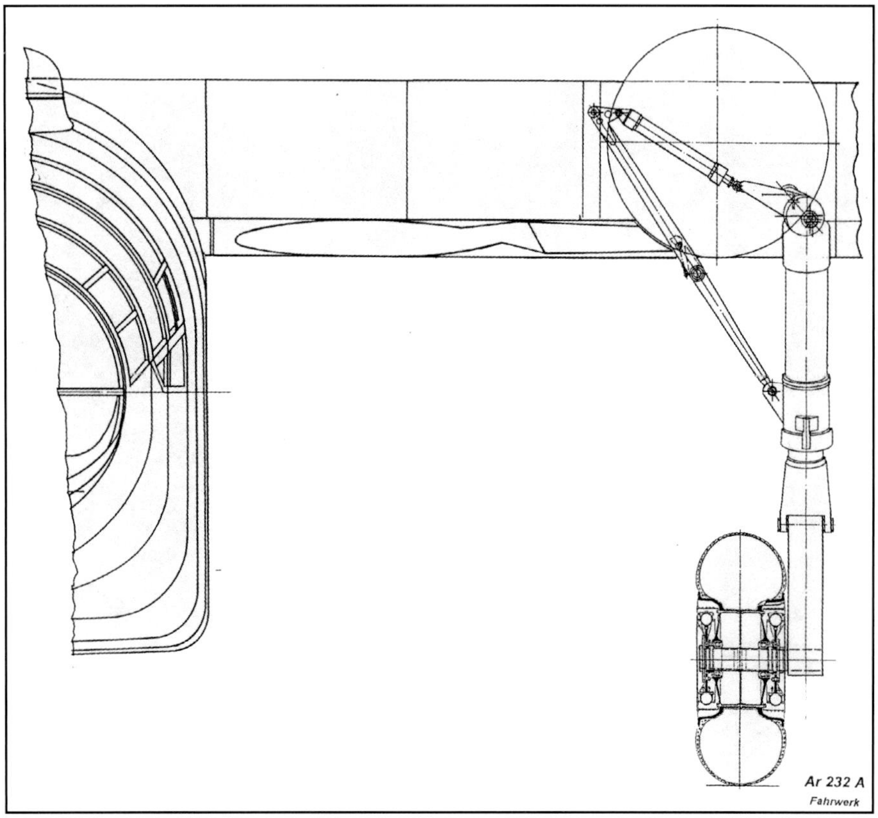

Main undercarriage seen from the front.
Drawing: Sengfelder

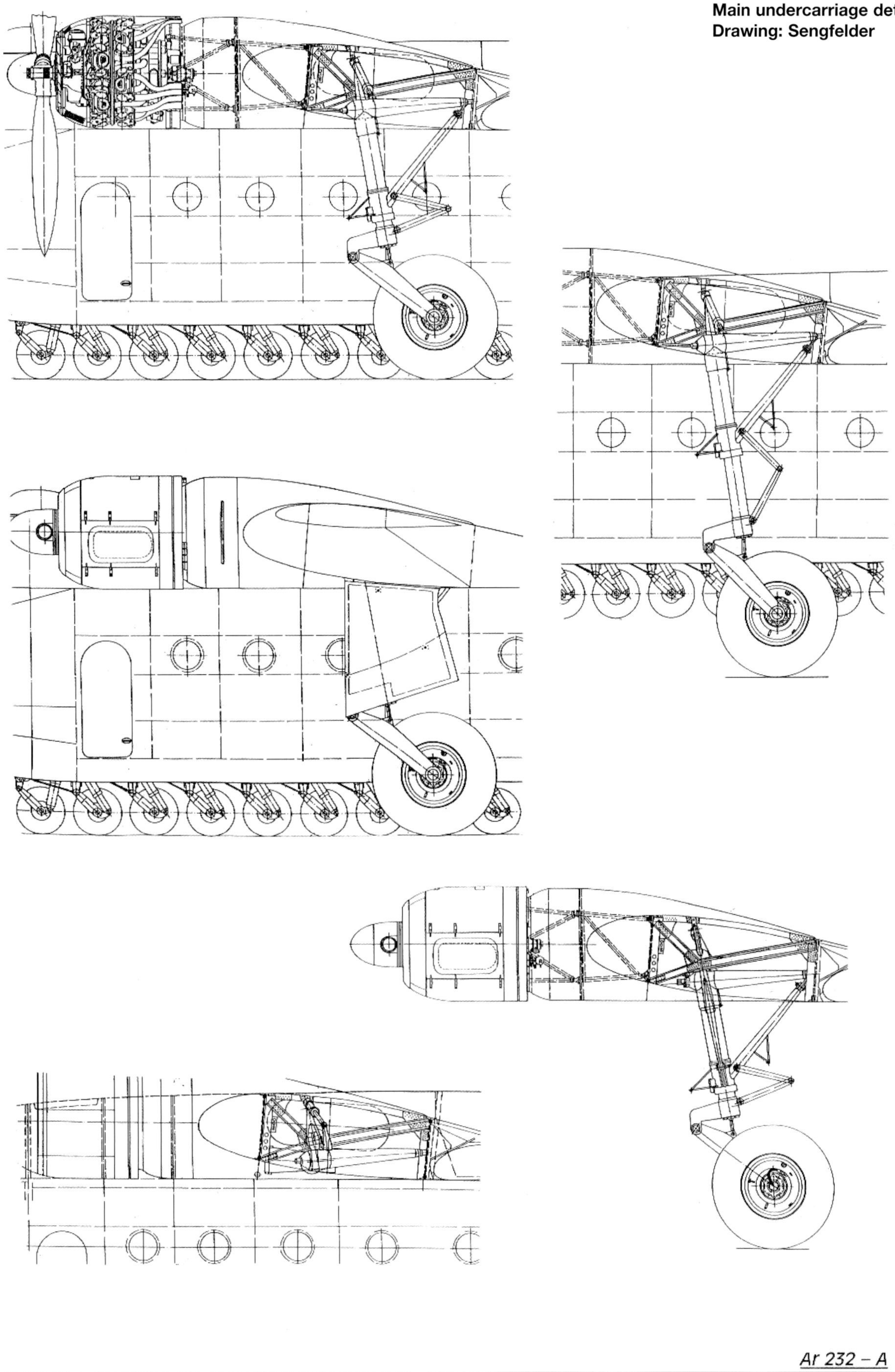

Main undercarriage details. Drawing: Sengfelder

Ar 232 – A

Close-up of the Arado Ar 232 illustrated on Page 4. The dorsal turret is clearly visible.

Photo: Andreas Klein Archive

TC+EE) was aborted due to poor weather in the target area. During the return flight the aircraft made an en route stop in Minsk and one of the main undercarriage legs collapsed. It turned out to be an act of sabotage, for an examination revealed that one of the bracing struts had been sawed through.

In preparation for a second flight using the Ar 232 B-05 (Werk-Nr. 011 0017, KI+ZX), three agents were dropped into the forests near Smolensk to scout landing sites. According to Soviet accounts, the radio operator defected and revealed the location of the landing site. The Soviet defense allegedly set up anti-aircraft guns and searchlights, in the event that the Germans became suspicious and tried to overshoot.

With the agents on board, the aircraft encountered heavy anti-aircraft fire before reaching the target area near Smolensk. As the weather was also unfavorable, the pilot decided to make a course change and on 4 September 1944 undertook a night landing at an alternate airfield near the village of Kuklovo. The aircraft sustained damage which was serious enough to prevent it from taking off again. After a Ju 88 was probably unable to locate the landing site, the crew was either taken prisoner or shot. The agents themselves were arrested by a patrol on 7 September while on their way to Moscow and were executed in 1952.

Another special operation under the leadership of KG 200 was the provision of Ar 232s in October 1944 to supply a German unit led by Oberstleutnant Scherhorn, which had become trapped behind Soviet lines. The plan was as follows:

> "After a landing site has been scouted and reported by Fähnrich Wild, four Arado Ar 232s, if possible in one night, will make a one-time delivery of supplies (20 tons) and fly out the badly wounded and those who cannot walk ... Further deliveries of supplies are planned during the withdrawal ... Air Fleet Command 6 requests approval of the planned missions and the temporary assignment of available Ar 232s (at least six) from VIX Air Corps to KG 200."

When the supply flights began on 8 December 1944, however, just two transports were available, probably the A-06 (Werk-Nr. 010 0008, G6+VY) and B-07 (Werk-Nr. 011 0029, G6+YY). Because of bad visibility, mechanical problems and enemy defenses, only a small quantity of supplies could be delivered by February 1945. After Scherhorn was captured, the operation came to nothing as a result of deception measures by the enemy.

At the beginning of March 1945 a number of Ar 232s moved to Tutow, where they were attached to 1./KG 200. Several of these later moved to Mühldorf. On 19 April 1945 one Ar 232 was sent to collect the wreck of a B-17 that had crashed in Manching. On 23 April two Ar 232s were sent to supply an encircled airfield near Zagreb. Toward the end of April, the last missions were flown from Tutow in support of army units attempting to crack the enemy ring around Berlin.

By the time the war ended most Arado transports had been lost, either shot down or destroyed by enemy fighter-bombers. An exception was the Ar 232 B-07, which had been part of "Operation Scherhorn". It fell intact into English hands in Eggebek. The others that survived were destroyed by their crews before they were captured. Among these was the Ar 232 A-05 (Werk-Nr. 010 0007, VD+YE), which had been retained by Arado. On 1 May 1945, just before the surrender, Walter Kroger had used it to fly company personnel from Warnemünde to Kaltenkirchen.

The multi-wheel undercarriage seen from behind.

Close-up of the multi-wheel undercarriage.

In 1943 in an "Elaboration on Development Lines", Arado had pressed Milch "to continue what Arado had begun", as "rough-field transports will also be useful in the future", none of the projected developments based on the Ar 232 got off the drawing board. The next planned development, the Ar 432, had the same engine layout and the cockpit and aft fuselage were the same as those of the Ar 232. There were only minor differences in dimensions. The cargo hold was supposed to be lengthened from 6.6 to 10 meters. Typical loads included half company consisting of 80 troops, eight anti-tank guns with 32 men, or three field howitzers with 18 men. Fuel capacity was supposed to be doubled. To achieve an acceptable wing loading, the wing center section was to be lengthened, resulting in a wing area of 165 m² compared to the 142.5 m² of the Ar 232 B. The increased weight would have made necessary larger wheels on the tricycle undercarriage.

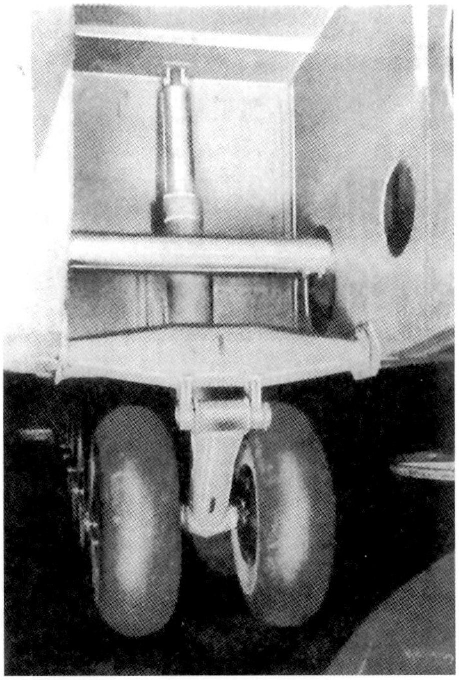

Start of the multi-wheel undercarriage behind the nosewheel bay.

One new consideration was that of also building the aircraft as a conventional transport without caterpillar undercarriage, with just a fixed tricycle landing gear. The payload of the Ar 432 rough field transport was 3200 kg. Without the weight of the caterpillar undercarriage (5000 kg) an airfield version of the aircraft would have had a greater payload than even the normal version of the Ar 432 in overload condition, meaning a landing on the tricycle undercarriage only (4600 kg).

Also decisive, of course, were the reduced materials consumption and production costs without the caterpillar undercarriage. After the startup of quantity production of the Ar 232 came under growing scrutiny on account of its technical complexity and use of high-value materials, over time proposed designs for the Ar 432 included reduced use of Dural through the use of replacement materials. As early as 6 November 1942, company director Walter Blume voiced the opinion that "even if many are skeptical about other materials, we must be prepared for 'orders' and undertake a changeover in materials now." Initial calculations revealed a radical substitute design using wood would result in, in some cases significant, reductions in the use of Dural and that the weight of completed aircraft would generally not be significantly greater.

The use of replacement materials in construction of the wing, tail section and parts of the fuselage of the Ar 432 was to be increased in stages. A general overview held out the prospect that the percentage of light metal used in the Ar 432 would be 38.2 percent, steel 42 percent and wood 19.7 percent. The percentage of wood was supposed to rise to 50% in the Ar 432 A-2. A design from August 1943 foresaw the use of 10.5 percent non-metallic materials, 14 percent wood, 29 percent light metal and 46 percent steel. It was envisaged that furniture makers would supply semi-finished wood products. As the use of steel as a replacement material in components weighing up to 500 kg was new in the aircraft industry and required a longer development period, negotiations were begun with Krupp and Eisenhütte Wissen.

The use of wood was initially concentrated in the outer wings. In a study on the design possibilities for a wooden outer wing, Hans Walland determined:

> "During a review of new transport designs, especially the wing of wood-steel mixed construction, I reached the conclusion that the design of the wooden outer wing should be as simple as possible, so that it can be made as light and torsionally stiff and as easy and cheap to produce as possible. Highly loaded and complicated installations (e.g. Fowler flaps and associated controls) should be avoided and relocated to the inner wing, whose load-bearing elements are more logically made of metal and therefore lighter. The transfer of larger forces into wooden wings is unpleasant and results in much uncertainty and weight."

An outer wing made of wood weighed 37 percent more than a Dural wing. As only simplified lift aids were available and the wing loading had to be correspondingly low, the wing area was to be greatly increased at the expense of a higher percentage of airframe weight to total weight. Walland proposed that the outer wing without Fowler flaps be developed as a double wing arrangement for both lateral control and high-lift and that the Fowler flaps on the inner wing be extended to the combined ailerons/flaps. This design promised a weight saving of about six percent and thus a 160 kg increase in payload.

The Ar 232 A-01 (VD+YA) photographed during takeoff in November 1942. The photos on this page clearly illustrate the different undercarriage positions for takeoff and landing (above) and rough-field operations (below).

These planned measures led to a considerable reduction in speed as well as climb and low-speed capabilities. Calculations by the design team revealed that with Fowler flaps extended 30%, the aircraft would be "completely unmanageable on account of serious longitudinal stability" and that rudder effectiveness would be seriously reduced. Another drawback of the new design was that, because of the absence of a joint, in case of a repair the outer wing could not be transported by rail. A "replacement wing" with joint, with which the aircraft could be flown to the factory, was suggested as a temporary expedient. The inner wing was envisaged as a steel tube framework in combination with Dural, with fabric skinning on the aft section. For the purpose of maintaining adequate statics while saving weight, the wing spar was to be carried through the fuselage, although this would hamper free movement in the cargo hold.

At a meeting on 12 May 1944, Milch gave the order for the "fastest possible plan for the

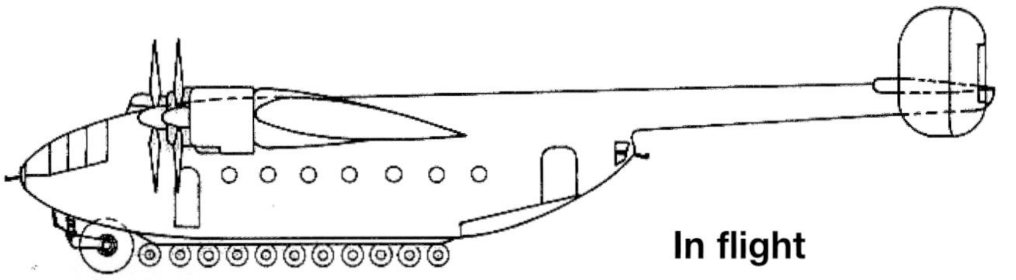

In flight

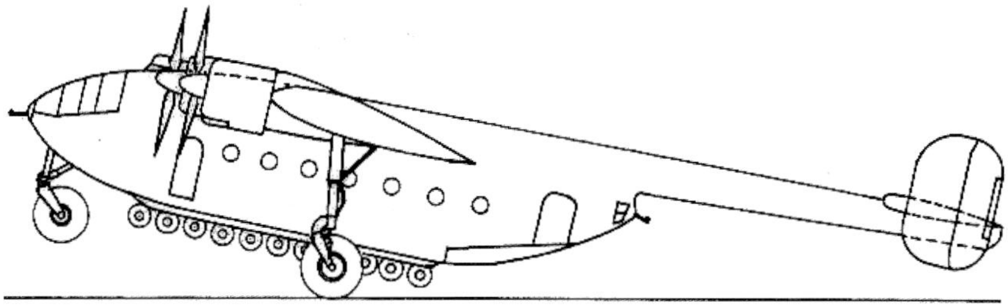

Touchdown and landing

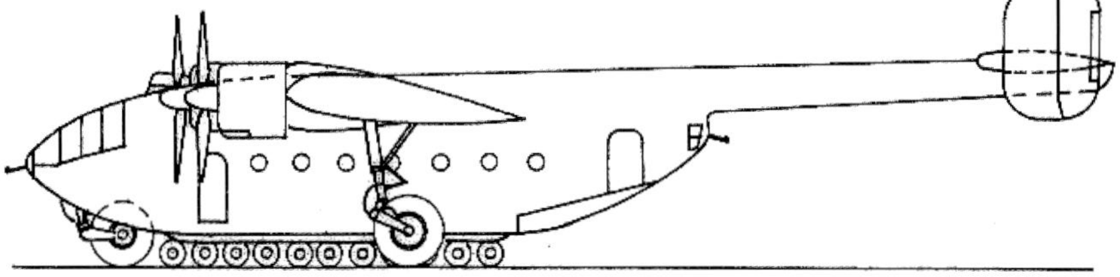

Rollout

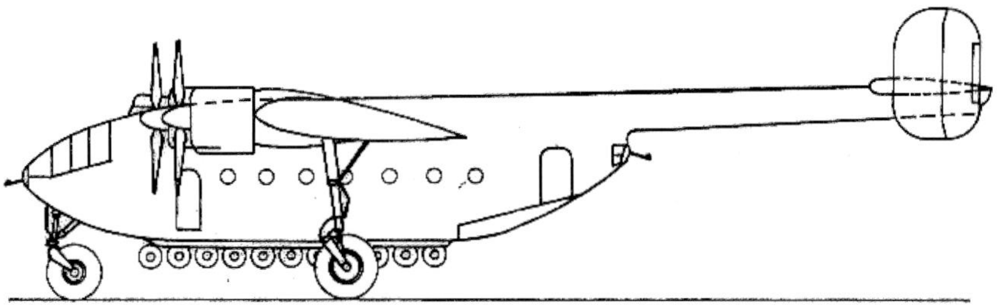

Taxiing on level ground

Taxiing on uneven ground

The Ar 232 A-01 (VD+YA) photographed after takeoff in November 1942.

Arado Ar 232 V2 (Werk-Nr. 232 0002) VD+YD during testing. The aircraft is finished in standard camouflage.

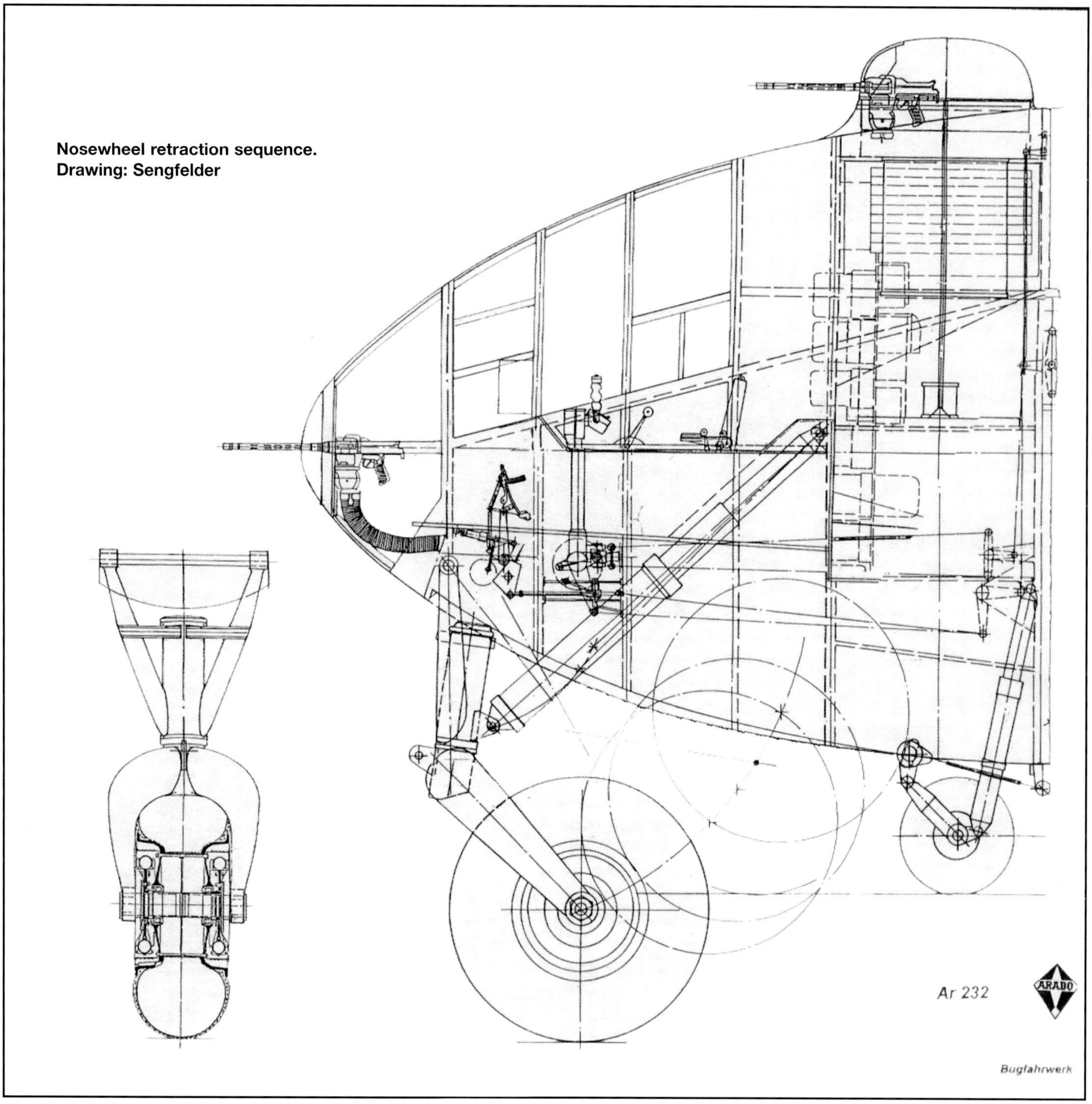

Nosewheel retraction sequence.
Drawing: Sengfelder

entire transport field and the quick startup of the Ar 432". In June 1944 there was another development meeting in Landeshut which was attended by Blume, almost all of the Arado department heads, and Amtschef GL/C-E Siegfried Knemeyer. It was decided that the wooden outer wing would undergo initial testing on a pre-production Ar 232 B-0. The minutes recorded the following plan:

"For lack of time, the aircraft will be delivered as they are in service with the units, but with wooden wings and wooden tail sections. The following test-beds are required for the test program:

- Ar 232 V1: replacement bearings testing
- B-02: testing of the dropping equipment (new floor)
- B-04: endurance testing of the airframe with wooden wing and tail
- B-011: control and handling characteristics testing
- B-010: testing for parachutists."

The Ar 432 A-01 and Ar 432 A-02 were scheduled for endurance testing of the ultimate design configuration and as a pattern aircraft for the desired series characteristics, respectively. A weekly report from Rechlin confirmed that in June 1944 the Ar 232 B-011 was being used by the company for pre-testing of the Ar 432. One of the first Ar 232

Ar 232 A-011 (Werk-Nr. 010 0012, TC+EG) of Westa 5, photographed near Spitzbergen, Norway in July 1943 (see color plate in fold-out section). The aircraft had sunk into the Polar soil, however the crew was able to upright it again.
Franz Selinger Archive

B-0 pre-production aircraft, probably fitted with a wooden wing and tail section, was one of the aircraft that took part in the last major demonstration of aircraft in Rechlin on 12-13 June 1944. A company memo dated 14 April 1944 noted that this aircraft had previously suffered a failure of the wooden tailplane and that reinforcement had been necessary as a result.

Following a meeting with the Reichsmarschall on 1 June 1944, several projects under development, such as the Ju 352, were cancelled, however the Ar 432 initially remained in the program. A planning overview dated 1 June 1943 reveals that production of the Ar 432 was supposed to begin in March 1944 despite the worsening production and materials situation. After

Ar 232 A-0 resting on its caterpillar undercarriage.
H.J. Ebert Archive

Ar 232 B-1 (Werk-Nr. 011 0013, KI+ZT) during assembly in the factory. Karl Kössler Archive

An Arado Ar 232 B-0. Photo: Hanfried Schliephake

Arado Ar 232 B-0. **Photo: Walter Zuerl**

delivery of the first aircraft in October 1944, production was to rise to a monthly maximum of 20 units in July 1945. Milch even considered increasing the monthly production rate to 70 aircraft after 1944. In addition, as a stop-gap an additional 21 Ar 232 B-0 transports were to follow the twentieth pre-production aircraft with the same production rate of three aircraft per month.

On 10 June 1944 it was decided that quantity production would end in October 1945. Blohm & Voss was to be mainly responsible for production. Production of individual components for the first two prototypes, which were probably not completed, began in Eger, where several Ar 232 A transports had been stationed in the winter of 1942-43. Soon afterwards, however, a meeting of department heads on 27 July 1944 resulted in the decision that "the Ar 432 will have to be further delayed, as there are insufficient workers available to work on the airframe and capacity for resources is temporarily entirely lacking." Construction of the Ar 432 thus moved into the distant future. The preparations for quantity production that had already been started had to be cancelled, as Arado was no longer receiving authorization for the procurement of materials. The same applied to the planned Ar 532 and Ar 632 large-capacity transports, whose gross weights were supposed to be between 26 000 and 30 000 kg.

During the planning phase for the Ar 432 a demand was made for an even more radical conversion to wood as a building material. In a study dated March 1943, Blume conceded that, in the course of materials conservation, he had been forced to fall back on construction methods from the 1930s. He regarded it, however, as an "advance in technology" that a "modern aircraft" could be developed from a "five-meter kite" from the time of the First World War. The latest technologies, such as boundary layer control, would be used to compensate for the inevitable constructive disadvantages. The study envisaged as its final goal to transport a payload of 4000 kg over a distance of 2000 kilometers in good takeoff and landing conditions with an aircraft that was to be two-thirds wood and which was supposed to surpass the performance of the Me 323 Gigant motorized large-capacity glider. It was to be capable of taking off

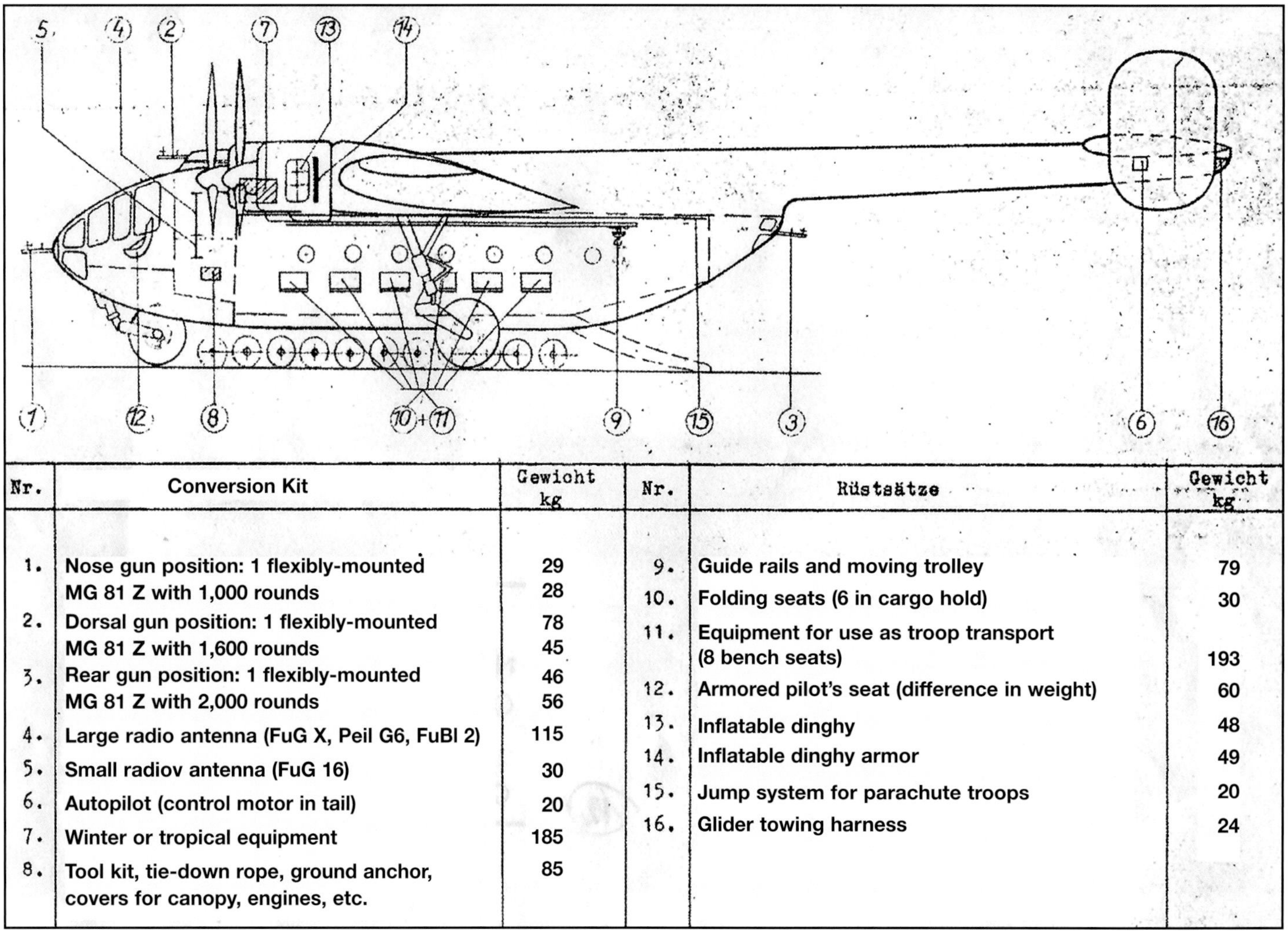

Nr.	Conversion Kit	Gewicht kg	Nr.	Rüstsätze	Gewicht kg
1.	Nose gun position: 1 flexibly-mounted MG 81 Z with 1,000 rounds	29 28	9.	Guide rails and moving trolley	79
2.	Dorsal gun position: 1 flexibly-mounted MG 81 Z with 1,600 rounds	78 45	10.	Folding seats (6 in cargo hold)	30
3.	Rear gun position: 1 flexibly-mounted MG 81 Z with 2,000 rounds	46 56	11.	Equipment for use as troop transport (8 bench seats)	193
4.	Large radio antenna (FuG X, Peil G6, FuBl 2)	115	12.	Armored pilot's seat (difference in weight)	60
5.	Small radiov antenna (FuG 16)	30	13.	Inflatable dinghy	48
6.	Autopilot (control motor in tail)	20	14.	Inflatable dinghy armor	49
7.	Winter or tropical equipment	185	15.	Jump system for parachute troops	20
8.	Tool kit, tie-down rope, ground anchor, covers for canopy, engines, etc.	85	16.	Glider towing harness	24

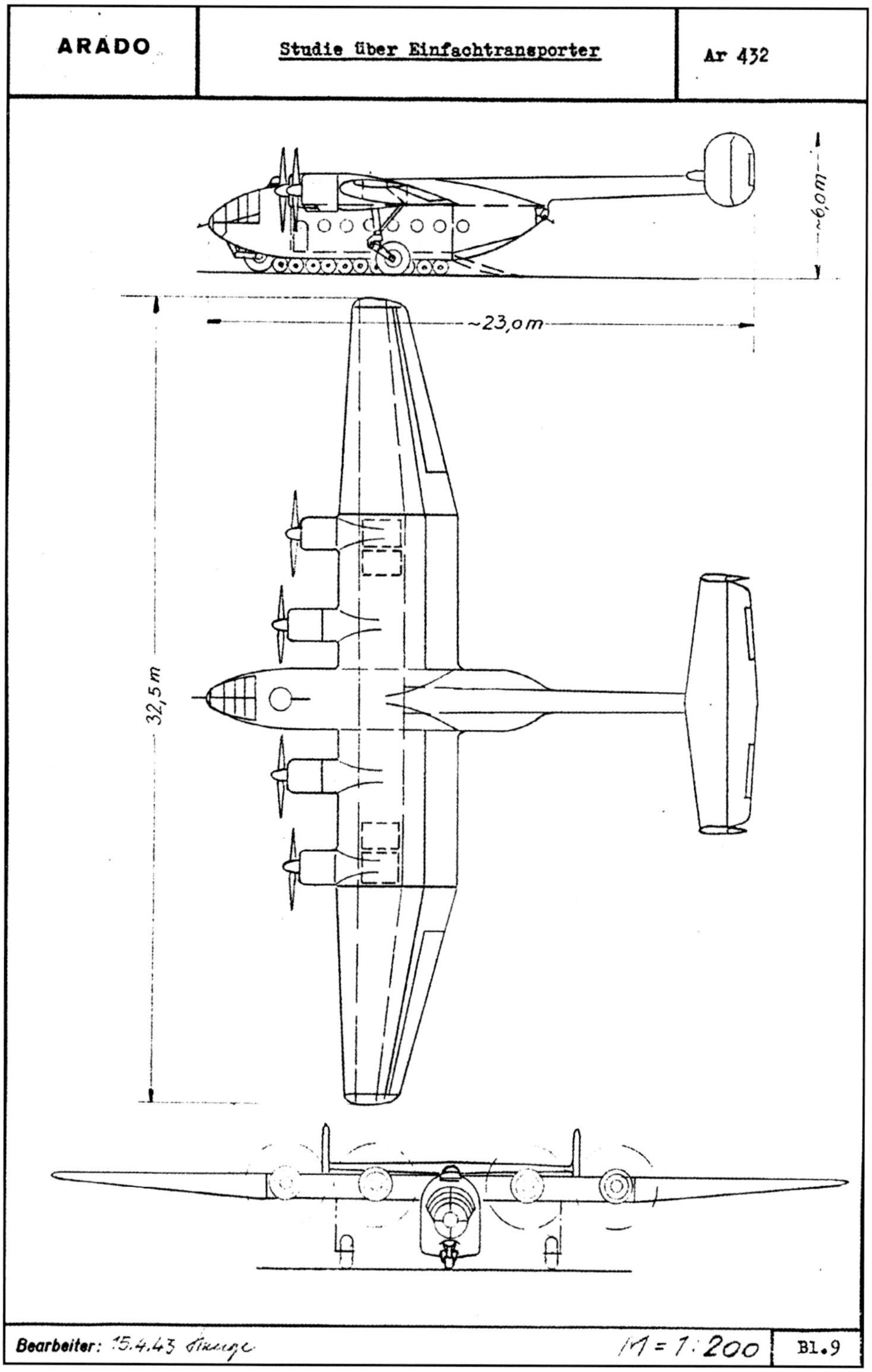

B-0 Series Specification

Wingspan	33,50m
Length	23,50m
Height	5,90m (lowered) 6,60m
Gross weight	20.000kg (overload)
Load capacity	7.170kg (overload)
Payload	4.650kg (overload)
Gross weight	17.500kg (normal load)
Load capacity	4.670kg (normal load)
Payload	2.150kg (normal load)
Maximum speed	312km/h
Cruise speed	255km/h
Landing speed	99km/h
Takeoff distance	350m (over 20m high obstacle)
Landing distance	157m
Service ceiling	6900m
Range	1335km
Power plant	4x BMW-Bramo 323 P mit 4x 1000PS 4x 810PS Kampfleistung
Armament	1x MG 81Z (A-Stand) 1x MG 131Z (B-Stand) 1x MG 81Z (C-Stand)

and landing distances of 300 meters. Other requirements: "fixed undercarriage, weak armament, most primitive construction, bare minimum of equipment".

According to a company memo dated 6 June 1944, Blume, in agreement with Siegfried Knemeyer, initiated the following steps to quickly bring the project to fruition:

> "TV and TB, together with HN, are to travel to the manufacturer as soon as possible for the purpose of assessing factory equipment and jig capacities."

On the same subject, he forcefully noted that it had been stated at the GL/ST Meeting "Wood" on 2 July 1944 "that significantly more wood must be put to use".

Arado was able to fall back on a related project study E 441-111 of May 1943, which envisaged a twin- or four-engined Ar 432 as a "simple transport", probably similar to the later Ar 432 B-1 and B-2. A three-engined version received no closer examination, as the Ju 352 was already designed for similar payload and range requirements. The aircraft was to be equipped with a fixed tricycle undercarriage exclusively. Compared to the Ar 432, the proposed twin-engined version was to have a reduced fuselage length (21 m vs. 23 m), greater wingspan (40 m vs. 33.5 m) and greater wing area (200 m² vs. 142 m²). The four-engined version was to have a fuselage length of 28 m, a wingspan of 45 m and a wing area of 310 m².

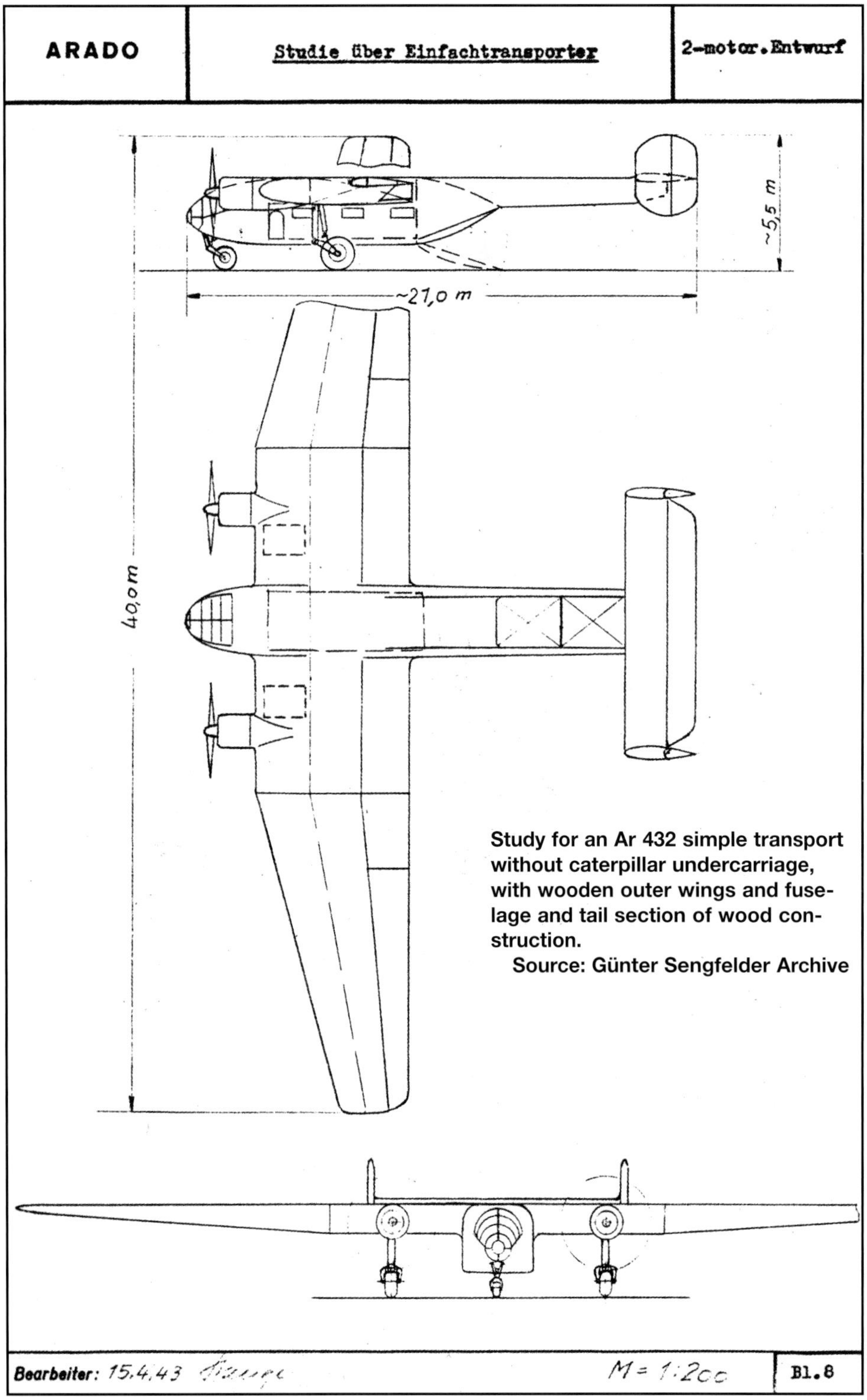

Study for an Ar 432 simple transport without caterpillar undercarriage, with wooden outer wings and fuselage and tail section of wood construction.
Source: Günter Sengfelder Archive

The wooden construction was to be extended to also include the cockpit, in the form of plywood skinning. As well, the entire cargo hold was to be made largely of wood. Plans called for a welded steel tube framework which, after installation of pine strips, was to be covered with fabric with a board surface in the floor area. The tail boom, originally designed as plywood tubes, was to be so fabricated that the side walls of the cargo hold, two flat frameworks of steel tube, would extend rearwards and be wire-braced against each other in the upper transverse fields. This would have caused the tail boom to lose its slim shape, however it would have provided a broader flat base for the tail section. After completion of the planning studies the result was not encouraging. Compared to the normal version of the Ar 432, the material cost of the twin-engined version fell from 90,000 RM to 60,000 RM. Production complexity increased significantly, however. At an assumed production of 150 aircraft per month, the number of man-hours required for airframe construction rose from 8,800 to 11,000 per aircraft. The cost of materials for the four-engined version was 70,000 RM, while the work load doubled. The four-engined simple transport was rejected because "the expenditure in labor and materials no longer has a healthy relationship to the required transport performance". Work on the twin-engined version was also halted because of inadequate performance. Climb performance was inadequate and the aircraft's weight, which could scarcely be reduced any farther, made single-engine flight impossible. As well, the amount of design work was such that deliveries of a simple transport could not be expected to begin before March 1946.

Book Translation by David Johnston.

Book Design by Stephanie Daugherty.

Library of Congress Control Number: 2011945952

Printed in China.
ISBN: 978-0-7643-4047-5

This book was originally published in German under the title *FLUGZEUG Profile 48, Arado Ar 232 "Tatzelwurm."*

We are interested in hearing from authors with book ideas on related topics.

Published by Schiffer Publishing Ltd.
4880 Lower Valley Road
Atglen, PA 19310
Phone: (610) 593-1777
FAX: (610) 593-2002
E-mail: Info@schifferbooks.com.
Visit our web site at: www.schifferbooks.com
Please write for a free catalog.
This book may be purchased from the publisher.
Try your bookstore first.

In Europe, Schiffer books are distributed by:
Bushwood Books
6 Marksbury Avenue
Kew Gardens
Surrey TW9 4JF, England
Phone: 44 (0) 20 8392-8585
FAX: 44 (0) 20 8392-9876
E-mail: Info@bushwoodbooks.co.uk.
Visit our website at: www.bushwoodbooks.co.uk

The captured Ar 232 B-07 (Werk-Nr. 011 0029, A3+RB) of 7./Erg.TG 7 wearing the Air Ministry number "17" at Farnborough in 1945.
Photo: DASA

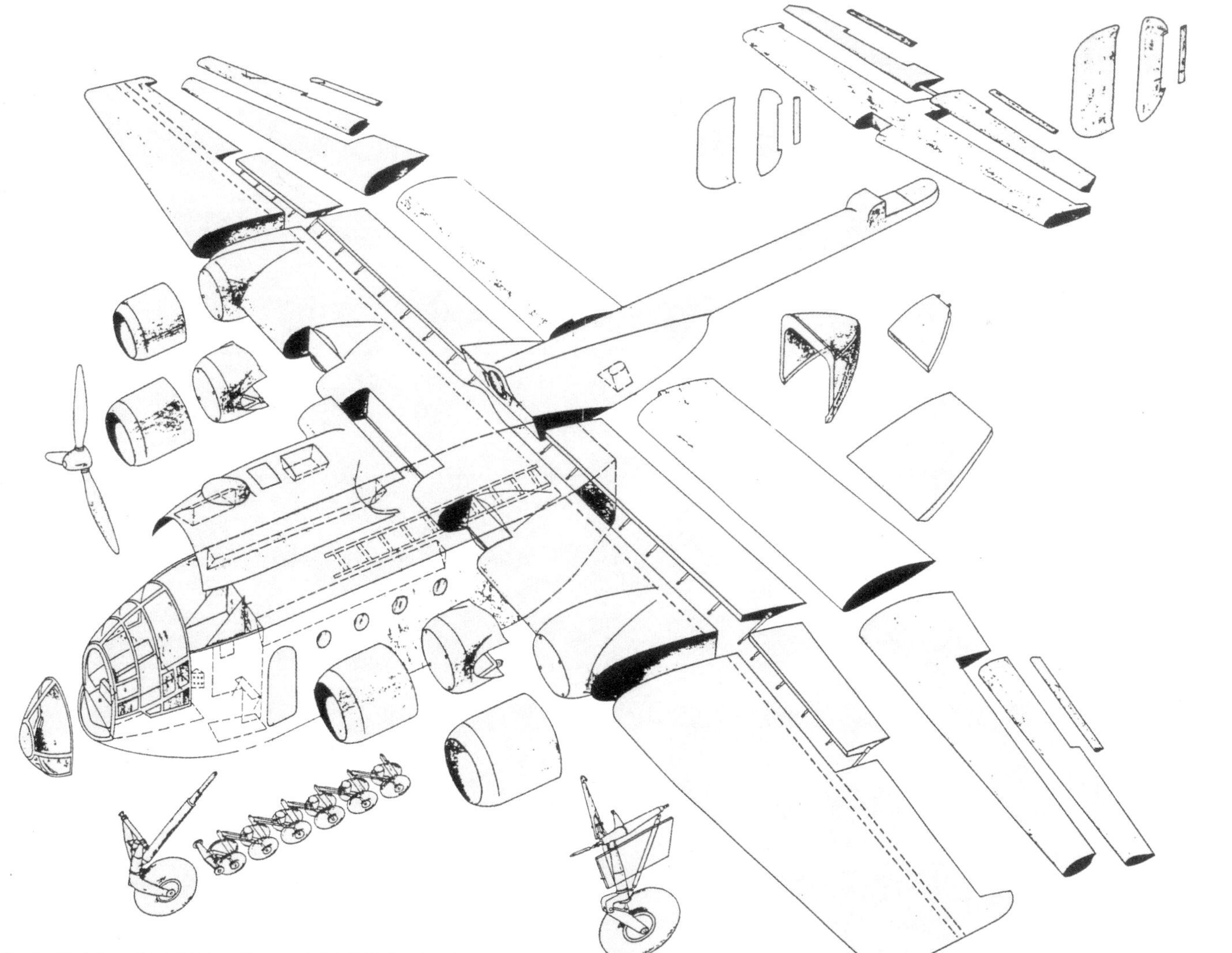

Exploded drawing of the planned Ar 432 A series.

The captured Arado Ar 232 B-07 at Farnborough. Note the "flying elephant", the Staffel emblem of 7./Erg.TG 7.

Other projects for transport and commercial aircraft by Arado had previously suffered the same fate as the Ar 432. The E 390 high-altitude airliner project of 1940 was quickly cancelled when the notion that the war would end soon turned out to be an illusion. The aircraft was to have had a pressurized cabin to enable economical operations at altitudes above 3000 meters. A trans-oceanic version for twelve passengers and a range of 6000 km was to have reached distant destinations like New York. Conceived at the same time as the E 390 high-altitude airliner, which was only envisaged for conversion into a transport, were the E 441 and E 470, both large-capacity transport aircraft. In terms of technology and capacity, they were on the edge of what was then possible. Typical were the designs' oversize wingspans of 47 to 68 meters, and the gigantic gross weights of between 88 000 and 157 000 kg. Derived from the E 233 project of 1940 was the Ar 430 twin-engined amphibious transport. Calculations and drawings for the wings and tail section were produced in 1941. After construction of a mock-up and tests in the water channel of the DVL's Institute for Marine Aviation in Hamburg, in 1943 the project was turned over to the French Dewoitine company. Beginning in April of the same year Sipa began delivering tail sections and landing flaps. Work on the project was halted in mid-1944 because of the military situation.

The same Arado Ar 232 B-07 at Farnborough, serving as backdrop for a souvenir photo of some British soldiers.

Photo: Klein Archive

Arado Ar 232 A-08 without code. Documents indicate that KG 200 used several aircraft for special operations. "Sumpfhuhn" (Moorhen) may have been one of these aircraft.